by

E.A. PARR B.Sc., C.Eng., M.I.E.E.

BERNARD BABANI (publishing) LTD
THE GRAMPIANS
SHEPHERDS BUSH ROAD
LONDON W6 7NF
ENGLAND

First Published – November 1980

British Library Cataloguing in Publication Data
Parr, Eric Andrew
Practical computer experiments
1. Microcomputers – Design and construction – Amateurs' manuals
I. Title
621.3819' 58' 35 TK 9969

ISBN 0 900162 98 8

Printed and Manufactured in Great Britain by Hunt Barnard Printing Ltd.

CONTENTS

1. INTRODUCTION

1.1 INTRODUCTION

According to what you read or who you listen to, the microprocessor will either lead us into the golden era of leisure or cause such a social upheaval that civilisation as we know it collapses. The reality will almost certainly be less extreme, but there is no doubt that the lives of each and everyone of us will be affected by the microprocessor in the years ahead.

Somewhat curiously, published material on the microprocessor tends to be of two sorts. The first treats the microprocessor as a black box and deals at length with programming and using the beast. The second type of book deals with the social impact, and at times I think more use has been made of the chip by social scientists than by electronic engineers. None of these books deal with the background to the chip, and this is a shame as the basic ideas are both interesting and simple.

This book is not intended as a guide to microprocessors, for this the reader is referred to the author's book "A Microprocessor Primer" also published by Bernard Babani (publishing) Ltd., Book No BP72. This book aims, rather, to fill in some of the background to the microprocessor by constructing typical computer circuits in discrete logic. It is hoped that the book will be a useful introduction to devices such as adders, stores etc. as well as a general source book of logic circuits.

1.2 ANALOGUE AND DIGITAL CIRCUITS

There are many ways that electronic circuits can be classified; amplifiers, oscillators, audio, video are common labels applied to specific circuits. A classification of interest to us is the division of electronics into analogue and digital circuits.

In an analogue circuit, voltages are not restricted in amplitude (other than the practical constraint of not overloading the circuit). In an audio amplifier, for example, the input can vary from a quiet woodwind passage to a loud rock group.

In a digital circuit, voltages can only take one of two states. Digital circuits are thus somewhat like switches which can be ON or OFF with no intermediate state, or a relay which can be either energised or de-energised. Typical analogue and digital units are:–

ANALOGUE	DIGITAL
Slide Rule	Electronic Calculator
Dial Watch	Digital Watch
Multimeter	DVM

An electronic circuit with only two states does not sound very useful. A single relay is not, of itself, capable of much control, but a panel full of relays can control complex machinery. Similarly several digital circuits can be made into a calculator or a computer. Fortunately digital circuits are well suited to integrated circuit manufacture, and very complex schemes can be made with just a few chips.

1.3 DIGITAL CIRCUITS

As stated above a digital circuit can only have two states. In the circuits described below we shall use a type of circuit called TTL. The initials stand for "Transistor Transistor Logic". In TTL the two voltage levels are 3.5v nominal and 0v nominal. These are known as '1' and '0' respectively.

It is not essential (or even desirable) to know what goes on inside a digital circuit, but for people who like to experiment the circuit of Fig. 1.1 is a good model of a TTL circuit called an inverter. The function of this circuit is simple; its output is the opposite state to the input. If the input is at 3.5v (1) the output will be at 0v (0) and vice versa.

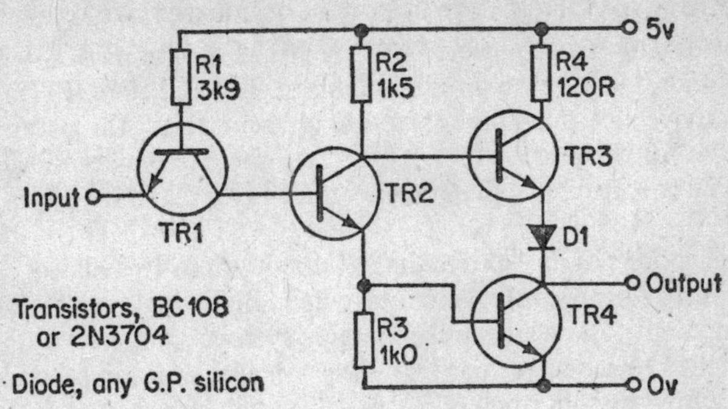

Fig. 1.1 Model of TTL inverter.

The operation of the circuit is fairly simple. With the input at 3.5v, TR2 is turned on by base current provided by R1 and TR1 base collector junction. TR4 is therefore turned on and the output pulled to 0v. With the input at 0v, TR1 is turned on, and TR2 turned off. Transistor TR3 acts as an emitter follower, pulling the output towards the positive supply.

TTL is not the only digital circuit. An equally popular type of digital circuit called CMOS is based on field effect transistors. The circuit of a CMOS inverter is shown on Fig. 1.2.

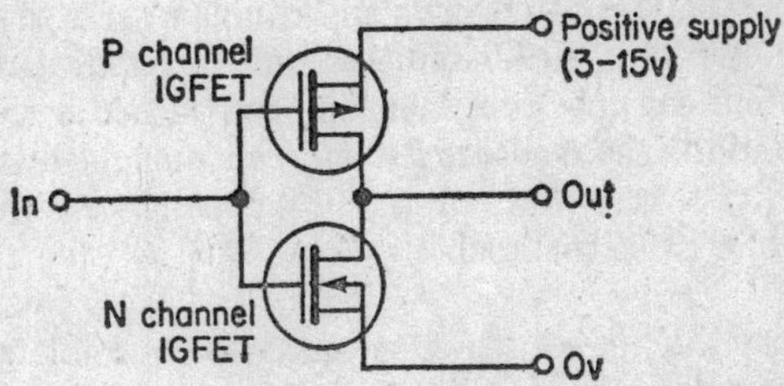

Fig. 1.2 CMOS inverter.

This is not the place to discuss the relative merit of TTL and CMOS in great detail. TTL is faster than CMOS but uses considerably more power. CMOS is ideal for running off batteries, but is more prone to damage. The ability of TTL to survive a certain amount of user abuse makes it the natural choice for the circuits in this book. All the circuits described can be constructed equally well with TTL or CMOS.

Applications of digital circuits fall roughly into two classes. The first class is control circuits, where digital logic controls equipment. These are similar to relay systems, and are designed to specifications like "Start air fan, wait ten seconds: if air flow present open pilot gas valve: wait one second, operate spark ignition for two seconds: if flame present open main gas valve: if not shut down and sound alarm"

The second class of digital circuit is concerned with arithmetic, and we shall see later that combinations of digital circuits can be used to represent numbers and perform arithmetic operations. These digital arithmetic circuits are the basis of electronic calculators and digital computers.

Initially we shall be concerned with digital circuits for control, as this is the easiest way to introduce the ideas of logic gates and similar functions.

1.4 CONSTRUCTIONAL NOTES

In the sections following many computer related circuits are described. These circuits are laid out such that the amateur can construct them and convince himself of their operation. The reader is strongly recommended to try the circuits, as one ounce of practical experience is worth one ton of written material.

The method of construction used will depend largely on the readers financial resources and the number of circuits he intends to attempt.

FIG.	7400	7402	7404	7406	7408	7414	7432	7442	7447	7473	7474	7475	7483	7486	7489	7490	7493	74121	74122	74125	74132	74147	74190	74194	555	ZN425E	Opto isolator	531 Op Amp
2.1				1																								
2.3				1	1																							
2.4				1	1																							
2.6				1			1																					
2.7				1			1																					
2.8				1	1																							
2.9			1	1	1																							
2.10			1	1			1																					
2.11	1			1																								
2.12	1			1																								
2.14				1										1														
2.17		1		1																								
2.18	1			1																								
2.20	1			1																								
2.22	1			1							1																	
2.23	1			1							1																	
2.25	1			1						1																		
2.26				1																					1			
2.27	1			1														1										
2.28	1																		1									
2.29				1															1						1			
2.30				1														1	1						1			
2.31				1		1																						
2.32				1		1																						
2.33	2		1	1														1										
3.1			1	1																		1						
3.2			1	1				1														1						
3.4			1	1				1	1													1						
3.5	1			1					1		2																	
3.6	1			1					1								1											
3.7	1			1					1							1												
3.8	1			1					1														1					
3.11	1													1														
3.12			2	1									1									2						
3.13			2	1									1	1								2						
3.15	1			1							2																	
3.16	1			1						2																		
3.17	1																							1				
4.3				2								3			1													
4.6	1			1																1								
4.8	1			2								5	1	1	1		1			5				1				
4.13				1																							1	
4.14																										1		
4.16				2																	1				1	1		1
TOTAL	2	1	2	2	1	1	1	1	1	2	2	5	1	1	1	1	1	1	1	5	1	2	1	1	1	1	1	1

Table 1 Summary of I.C.P.s required.

Fig. 1.3 Typical general purpose P.C.B.

Table 1 lists the i.c.p.s. necessary for each experiment and summarises the total number of chips necessary for every experiment to be attempted. The ideal construction method is to use one of the i.c.p. G.P. boards similar to Fig. 1.3. If this is equipped with 14 pin sockets and 16 pin sockets along with 7406s arranged as monitors (described in section 2.1), every circuit can be built. Each pin on a socket is brought out to a terminal pin, and connections can be made by point to point wiring as shown on Fig. 1.4. Each pin then has no more than 2 wires connected to it.

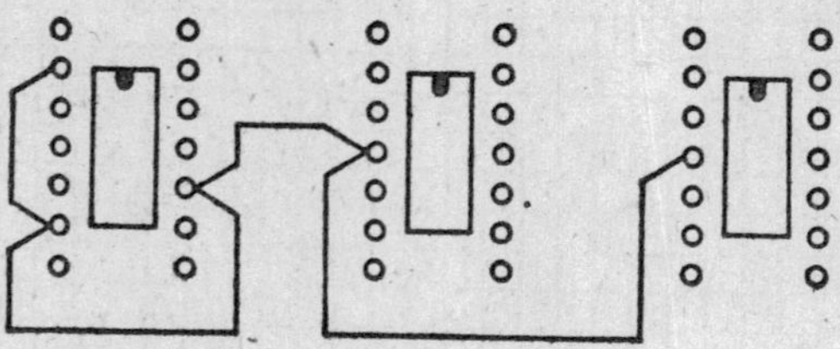

Fig. 1.4 Point to point wiring.

A more ambitious project might be considered if the experiments are to make part of an educational project. A case could be constructed with a lid denoting various logical functions, with inputs and outputs brought out to 1mm sockets (see Fig. 1.5). The circuits are then constructed by means of jumper leads with 1mm plugs. This approach allows for easy construction of circuits, but is expensive both in initial time and construction costs.

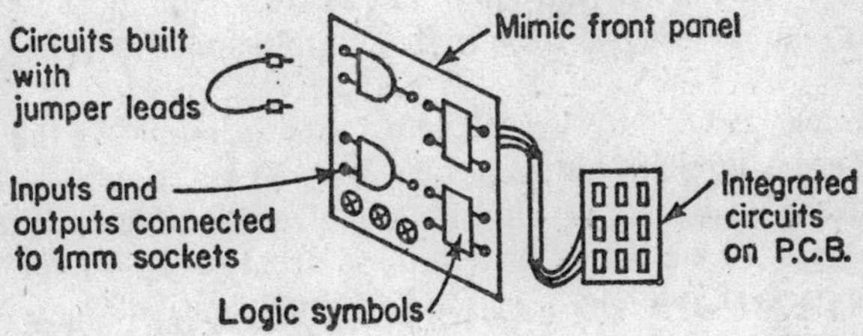

Fig. 1.5 Demonstration system.

The simplest method would be to construct each circuit as a "one-off". This would be practical if a few circuits were to be attempted, but prohibitively expensive for any significant number.

Whichever constructional method is used, some care must be taken with the wiring. All logic circuits operate at high speed, with fast edges of typically a few nanosecs rise and fall time. At these speeds effects too complex to discuss in a book of this size can cause reflections to occur under some circumstances. These reflections cause one single pulse to appear at the receiving end as several pulses. In general, reflections can be avoided if all connecting wires are kept below 300cms in length. One rule, therefore, is KEEP ALL WIRES SHORT.

A related effect is crosstalk. If two wires are run parallel for any distance, coupling between wires can cause faulty signals to be induced from one wire to its neighbour. This, again, is caused by the high operating speed of logic circuits, and can be avoided by not using long parallel wires.

As logic circuits operate, current pulses are caused as gates switch. These current pulses induce voltage spikes on the power supply leads. Each and every chip should therefore be decoupled by a 0.1μF capacitor across the supply pins, and the power supply leads made as short as possible.

These elementary precautions should be taken in all logic circuits, whether in this book or elsewhere, and in most circumstances will give freedom from problems with noise.

The integrated circuits we will be using are packaged in the familiar beetle shaped Dual in Line Pack. These come commonly in 14 pin, 16 pin and 24 pin versions. Viewed from above, pin 1 is on the left hand side adjacent to the cut out in the package (see Fig. 1.6). Pin 1 is often identified by a small circle.

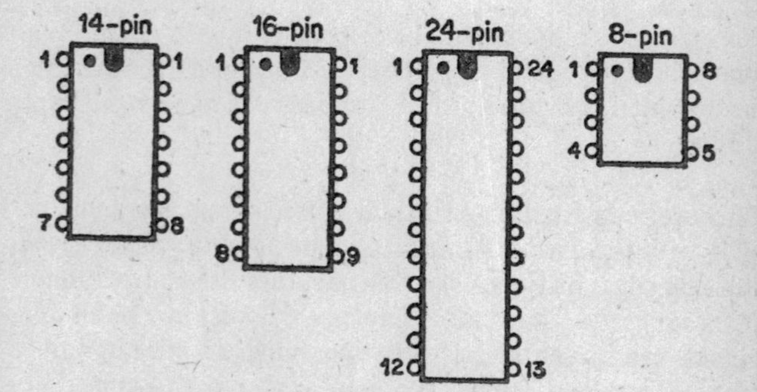

Fig. 1.6 Dual-in-line packages.

Most circuits require some switches or pushbuttons. Unfortunately switches are more expensive than i.c.p.s, and new switches will be a major item in the cost of the projects. There are, fortunately, several cheaper alternatives.

In several circuits, a simple flying croc clip lead will suffice (see Fig. 1.7) with solder pins for contacts. This is probably the cheapest way of implementing a switch. An alternative is to purchase ex-Army or ex-GPO switches from surplus stores. Post Office key switches are particularly well suited for these projects, and are often available ready mounted in rows. Model Railway magazines often advertise cheap switches.

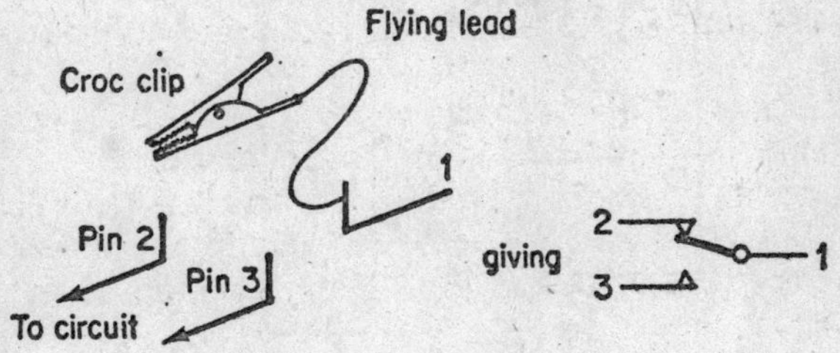

Fig. 1.7 Cheap croc clip switch.

1.5 POWER SUPPLY

Our logic experiments are to be done with TTL which requires a 5 volt supply. Fortunately it is very easy to construct a suitable supply using the readily available integrated circuit regulators.

A suggested circuit is shown on Fig. 1.8. This will supply 5 volts at 1 Amp which is more than adequate for all the circuits described in this book. Rectifier D1 and capacitor C1 produce a smoothed D.C. voltage of about 10 volts. The i.c.p. is a complete series regulator giving the 5 volts required. Capacitors C2 and C3 remove ripple on the output, and resistor R1 provides a minimum load.

It is essential, for safety reasons, that the circuit be built in an earthed metal case, and normal precautions taken when testing the circuit. Ideally the 10v, 5v and 0v connections should be brought out to terminals on the box lid to permit easy connections to the circuit under construction.

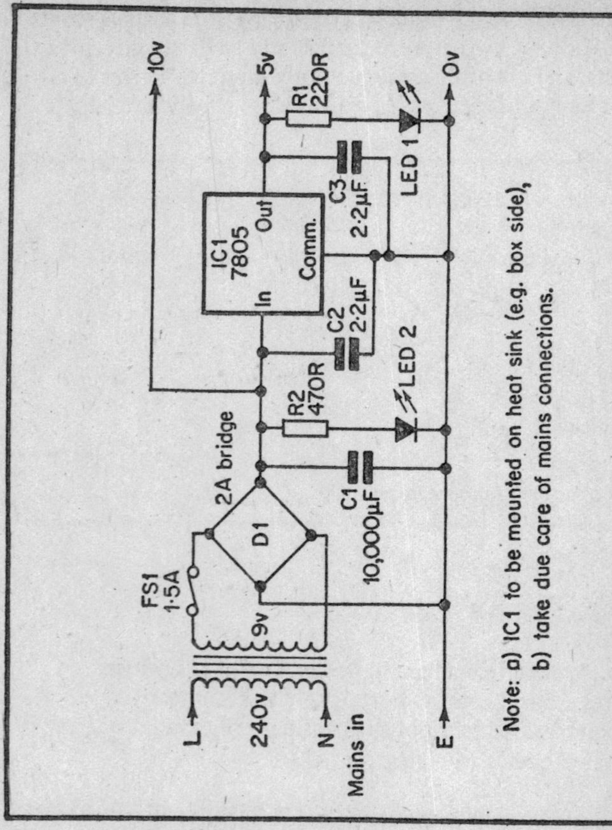

Fig. 1.8 Power supply.

R1, LED1 and R2, LED 2 provide a useful, but not essential, indication of supply presence or absence.

If the regulator i.c.p. is bolted to a reasonable heatsink (such as the box wall) the circuit will withstand a prolonged short circuit. Note that the heatsink on the regulator is connected to 0v, so no insulating washers are required.

The transformer and D1 could be replaced by a 9 volt battery if preferred, but battery life will be somewhat restricted. The 5 volt PSU described above should be used if possible.

2. CONTROL CIRCUITS

2.1 STATE INDICATOR

We will need to monitor the state of various points within the circuits we are going to build. In many circuits we will need to monitor several points simultaneously, and it would obviously be prohibitively expensive to use several multimeters. Fortunately in a logic circuit only two states can exist, binary '0' and binary '1', so we do not need analogue indicators. A cheap and simple 6 point monitor can be made using a 7406 hex inverter; 6 LEDs and 6 resistors as shown on Fig. 2.1.

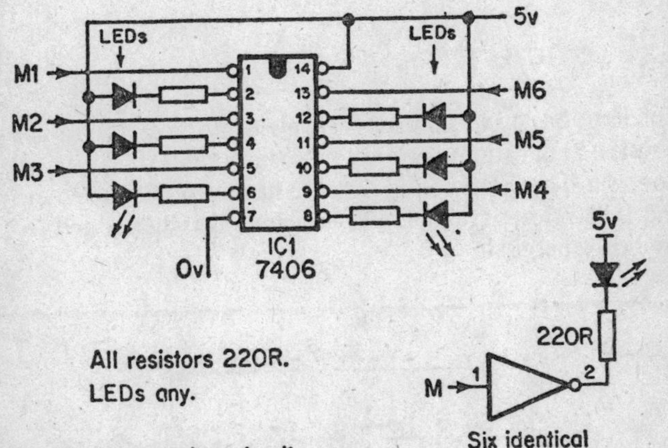

Fig. 2.1 Hex monitor circuit.

The operation of this is simple. An inverter gives a '0' out for a '1' in, and vice versa. When the output of an inverter is at a '0', current will flow through the LED causing it to glow. The resistor limits the current to a safe value. The LED will thus light when the input is at a '1'. The circuit of Fig. 2.1 thus provides cheap indication of 6 points. The construction of such circuits will cover the requirements of all the circuits in the book. In the circuit diagrams following the letter M denotes a monitor point to which an indicator should be connected.

After construction, flying leads should be connected to the six inputs and the 5v and 0v connections made to the power supply. With an input disconnected or connected to 5v the corresponding LED should be on. When an input is connected to 0v the LED should go out.

Commercial logic monitors are available similar in principle to the circuit above. A very useful device is the clip on probe which attaches direct to an i.c.p. and shows the states of all pins. Devices similar to pencils are also available. These devices generally distinguish between a '0', '1' and float unlike our simple indicator.

2.2 LOGIC GATES

The most basic and simplest logic elements are gates. In the simplest applications they can be used to replace relays. Consider the circuit of Fig. 2.2. We have two relay contacts A and B in series, so relay C will energise only when A and B are both energised.

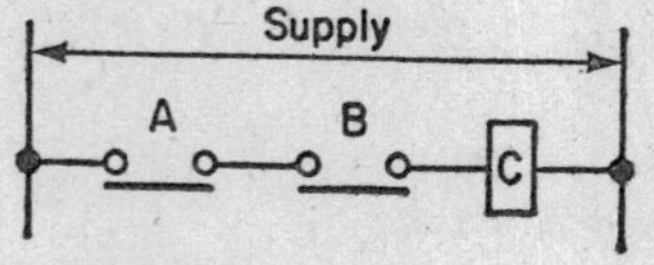

Fig. 2.2 Relay AND gate.

Using a 7408 AND gate, we can duplicate the operation of the relay circuit. Using 2 switches, 3 monitors and a 7408 gate we can set up the circuit of Fig. 2.3. The two switches SWA and SWB give a '1' when they are switched to 5v and a '0' when they are switched to 0v.

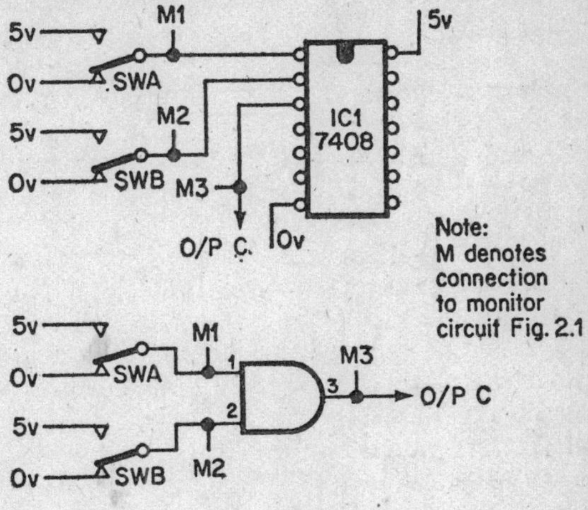

Fig. 2.3 AND gate circuit.

There are four possible combinations of inputs, detailed below. The reader should try all these, and fill in the resulting outputs in the table. Remember that M3 will be lit for a '1' out.

SWA	SWB	Output C
0	0	
0	1	
1	0	
1	1	

You should find that you get a '1' out only when both inputs are at '1'. In the other 3 cases the output is a '0'.

The gate is thus analogous to the relay circuit of Fig.2.2 above.

AND gates are available with more than 2 inputs; 3, 4, and 8 input gates being common. We can simulate the action of a 3 input gate by the circuit of Fig. 2.4. It will be found that the output is a '1' only when all three inputs are at a '1'.

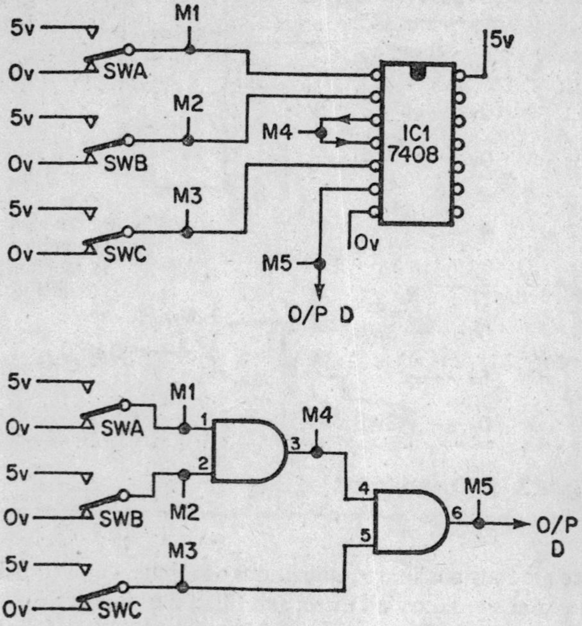

Fig. 2.4 Simulation of 3-input AND gate.

The next gate is similar to the parallel relay circuit shown on Fig. 2.5. Relay C will be energised when either relay A or relay B is energised. Not surprisingly the corresponding logic gate is known as an OR gate.

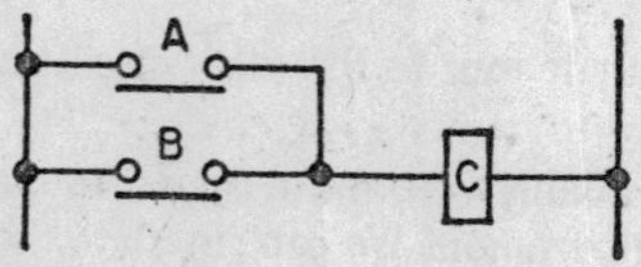

Fig. 2.5 Relay OR gate.

The operation of an OR gate can be demonstrated by the circuit of Fig. 2.6. Note that the wiring is identical to Fig. 2.3. If sockets have been used, a simple chip replacement is all that is required. There are again 4 combinations of inputs, and the reader should record the results below. Again remember that a monitor is lit for a '1'.

SWA	SWB	Output C
0	0	
0	1	
1	0	
1	1	

The output C should be at a '1' if either, or both, inputs are at a '1'.

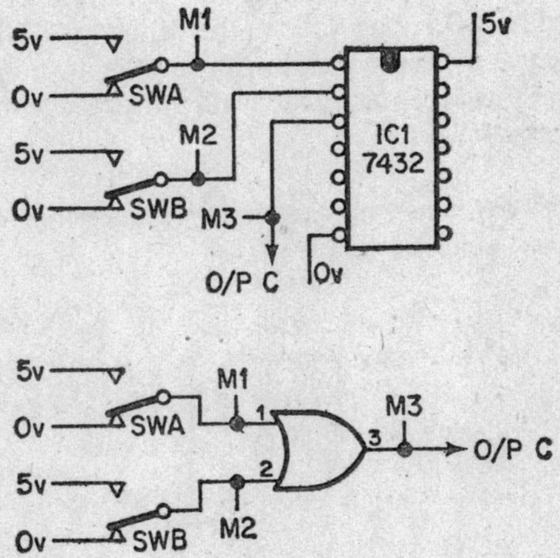

Fig. 2.6 Demonstration circuit for OR gate.

OR gates can, again, be obtained in 3, 4, or 8 input forms Fig. 2.7 shows the implementation of a 3 input OR gate.

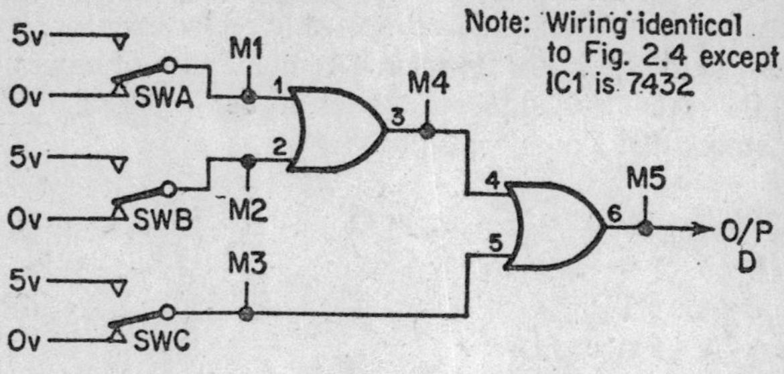

Fig. 2.7 Simulation of 3-input OR gate.

The next gate is the inverter. We have already utilised the inverter in our monitor, but we can now look at its operation in detail. An inverter gives a '1' out for a '0' in and vice versa, as demonstrated by the circuit of Fig. 2.8. If sockets are being used on a G.P. board, leave the wiring used for the AND and OR gate experiments, and construct the inverter circuit on another socket. Later circuits will utilise the wiring of Fig. 2.3 and 2.8..

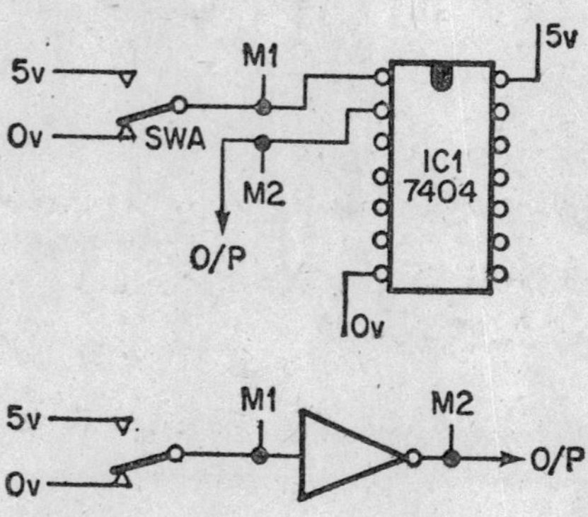

Fig. 2.8 The inverter gate.

There are only two possible states, and it should be found that the output will be the opposite state to the input.

Input M1	Output M2
0	
1	

The next gate is called the NAND gate, and is in reality an AND gate followed by an inverter. It can be simulated by the circuit of Fig. 2.9 using the 7408 AND gate followed by the 7406 inverter used previously.

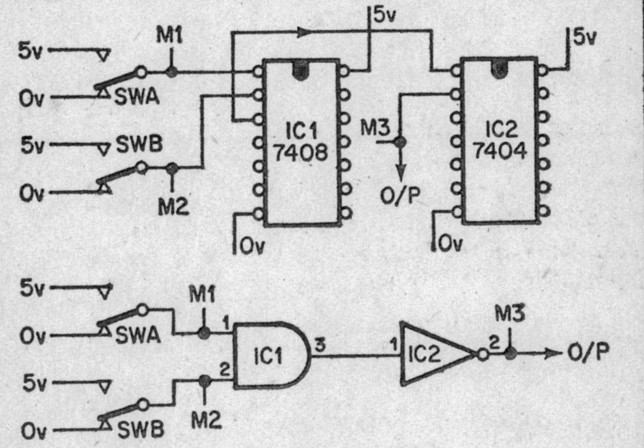

Fig. 2.9 Simulation of NAND gate.

The four possible input combinations should again be tried, and the results recorded.

SWA	SWB	Output M3
0	0	
0	1	
1	0	
1	1	

It should be found that the output is at a '0' if, and only if, both inputs are at a '1'. Otherwise it is at a '1'. Compare this with the circuit for the AND gate tried previously.

We can also have a NOR gate, which is an OR gate followed by an inverter. This can be demonstrated by the circuit of Fig. 2.10 (note that the wiring is the same as Fig. 2.9, only IC1 is changed). The four results should again be recorded.

SWA	SWB	Output
0	0	
0	1	
1	0	
1	1	

Compare this with the results obtained for the simple OR gate.

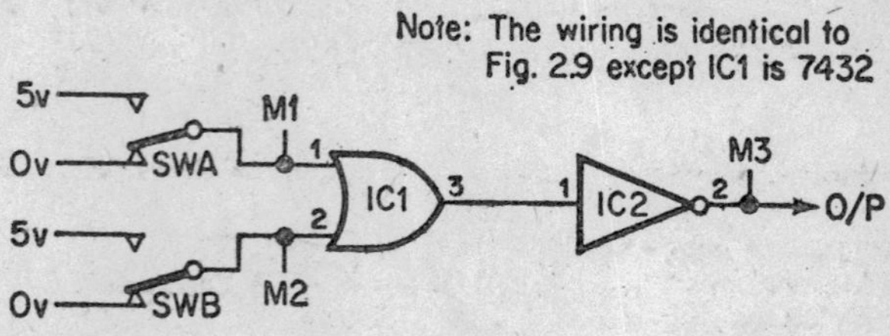

Fig. 2.10 Simulation of NOR gate.

The NAND gate and NOR gate are encountered more often than any other gate, and are available in i.c.p.s. The commonest i.c.p. is probably the 7400 quad NAND gate, shown on Fig. 2.11. The results for this gate should be recorded below.

SWA	SWB	Output
0	0	
0	1	
1	0	
1	1	

The results should be identical to those obtained for Fig. 2.9.

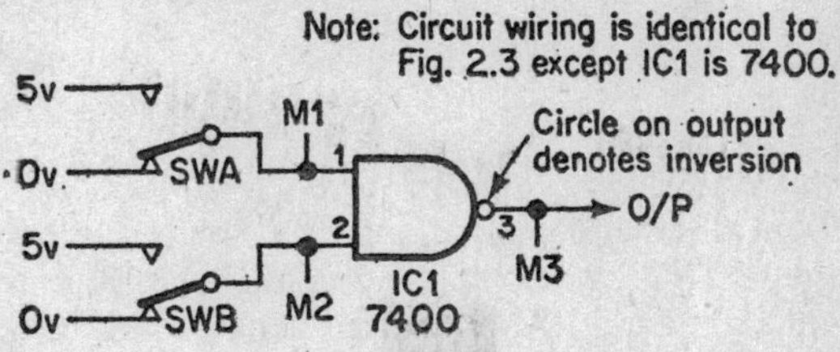

Fig. 2.11 Demonstration of NAND gate.

The use of NAND gates and NOR gates might seem an unnecessary. complication, but in practice they are more versatile than simple AND and OR gates. This can be demonstrated by the circuit of Fig. 2.12. There are 16 input combinations, and the reader should try them all to see if he can deduce the relationship between the output and the four inputs.

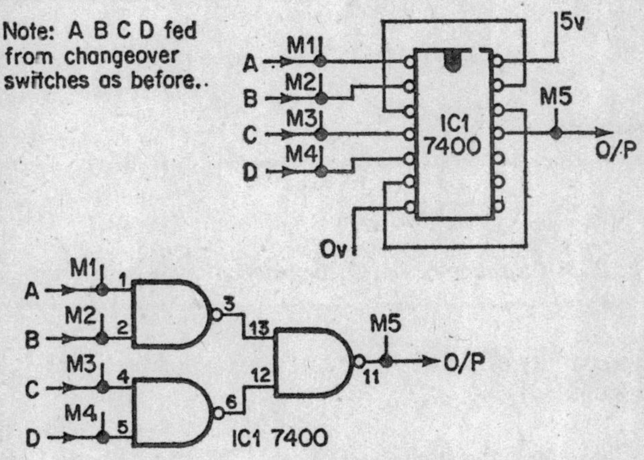

Fig. 2.12 Demonstration of versatility of NAND gate.

If the circuit is operating correctly, you should get:—

A	B	C	D	Output
1	1	0	0	1
0	0	1	1	1
1	1	1	1	1

and '0' in all other combinations. The circuit thus behaves like the AND/OR gate combination of Fig. 2.13. In some odd way the right hand NAND gate has behaved like an OR gate. The reason for this can be found in the results for a NAND gate obtained previously. With both inputs at a '1' we get a '0' out. Conversely, we could say that any input going to a '0' will cause the output to go to a '1' If we were to define a '0' as 5v and a '1' as 0v, the NAND gate would be a NOR gate (don't worry if you have to read that several times to grasp it!). This is effectively what is happening in Fig. 2.12. The two left hand gate outputs will go to a '0' when both their respective inputs are at a '1'. If either of the outputs goes to a '0' the output of the right hand gate will go to a '1', as we found by experiment.

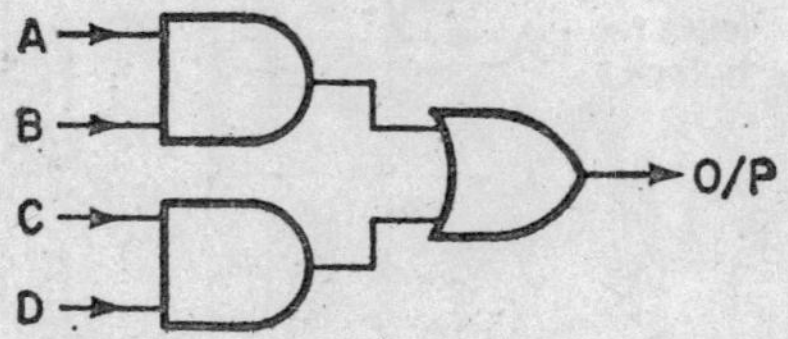

Fig. 2.13 Operation of NAND combination above.

This versatility of NAND and NOR gates is the reason for their popularity.

The final gate is the exclusive OR gate. This can be investigated with the circuit of Fig. 2.14. Note again that the same wiring is used. The results should be recorded below.

SWA	SWB	Output
0	0	
0	1	
1	0	
1	1	

The results should show that the output is a '0' when the inputs are the same, and a '1' when the inputs are different.

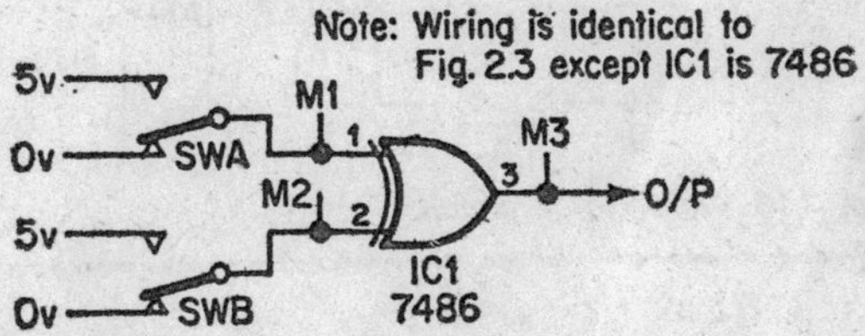

Fig. 2.14 Demonstration of exclusive-OR gate.

We have described six basic logic gates. These gates are the building blocks on which all logic and computer systems are built. The gates are all shown on Fig. 2.15.

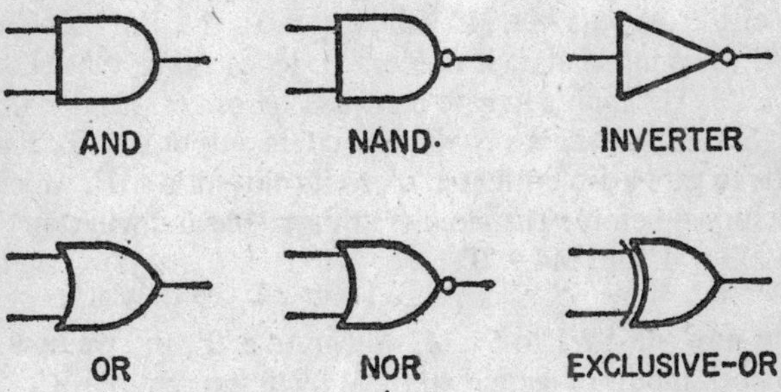

Fig. 2.15 Summary of logic gates.

2.3 MEMORIES

In logic systems, it is often necessary to remember that something has happened. This is achieved by logic circuits known as "Memories". There is a direct analogy in the relay circuit of Fig. 2.16 which is often used to start and stop electric motors.

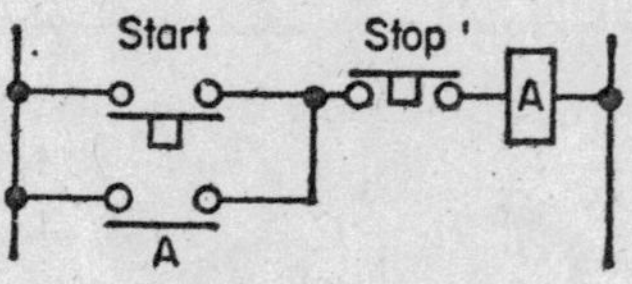

Fig. 2.16 Relay latch circuit.

When the start push button is pressed, RLA will energise, and the contact of RLA will maintain current to the coil when the push button is released. The relay thus stays energised. If the stop push button is now pressed, the relay de-energises and will stay de-energised when the stop button is released. The circuit thus remembers which push button was pressed last.

We can build a logic memory circuit with two NOR gates as shown on Fig. 2.17. In the quiescant state, both SW1 and SW2 should be set to 0v. On power up, one, and only one, of the outputs M3, M4 will be at a '1', the other will be at a '0'. The initial state is random, so let's assume that M3 is at a '1'. The inputs to gate b are a '1' (from M3) and a '0' from SW2. The gate is a NOR gate, so its output is a '0'. The inputs to gate a are both at a '0', so its output is a '1', which we assumed before. The circuit is thus stable and will stay with M3 = '1' and M4 = '0'.

Let us now put SW1 to 5v. M3 will go to a '0', and we now have both inputs on gate b at '0'. M4 will thus go to a '1'. The outputs M3 and M4 have changed state. If SW1 is returned to 0v, the circuit will stay with M4 = '1' and M3 = '0'.

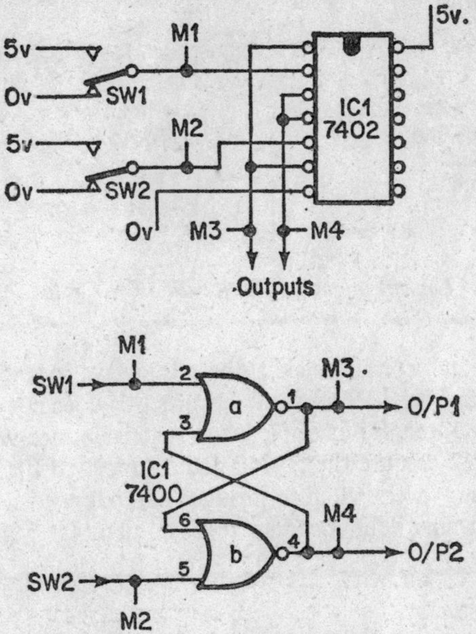

Fig. 2.17 Logic memory circuit with NOR gates.

Operation of SW2 from 0v to 5v back to 0v will change the circuit back to its original state. The circuit thus remembers which switch was last at a '1' position.

As an exercise the reader should try to work out what would happen if both SW1 and SW2 are set to 5v, and see if the circuit behaves as expected. In logic systems, the circuit is usually designed so that both inputs cannot go to a '1' together.

It is also possible to design a memory with NAND gates as shown on Fig. 2.18. This circuit remembers which input went to a '0' last. Note that the pinning of Fig. 2.17 and Fig. 2.18 are similar, so the 7402 NOR chip can simply be replaced by a 7400 NAND to give Fig. 2.18.

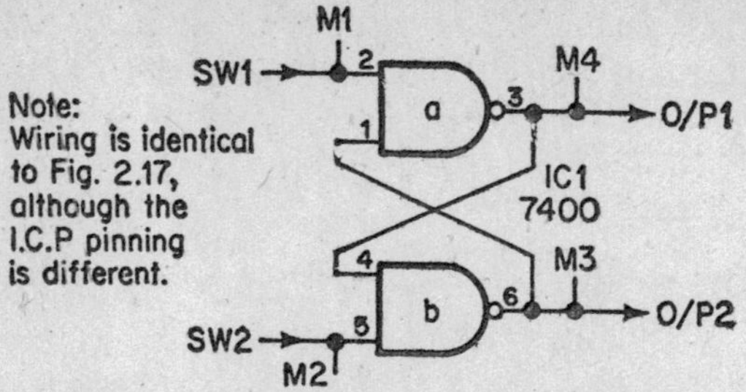

Fig. 2.18 Logical memory circuit with NAND gates.

When a switch contact makes, there is always contact bounce as shown in Fig. 2.19. In some circuits this does not matter, but in a counter, for example, each switch bounce will be counted. We can use the NAND gate memory of Fig. 2.20 with a changeover switch to produce a debounced signal. We shall use similar debounced switches in many later circuits.

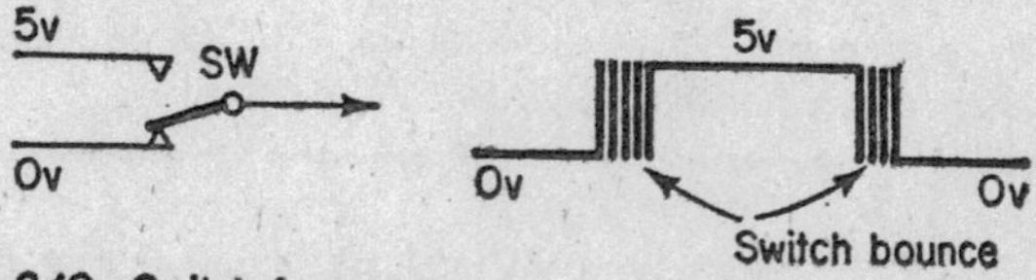

Fig. 2.19 Switch bounce.

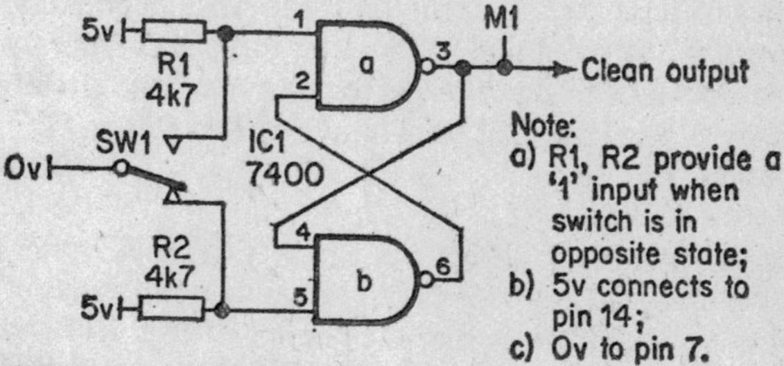

Fig. 2.20 Switch debouncing.

The memories in Fig. 2.17 and Fig. 2.18 are known as S-R flip flops. These are the simplest memory circuits, and there are two other common memories. The first of these is the D type flip flop shown on Fig. 2.21. This has two inputs labelled D (for data) and CK (for clock). There are two outputs usually labelled Q and $\overline{Q}$.

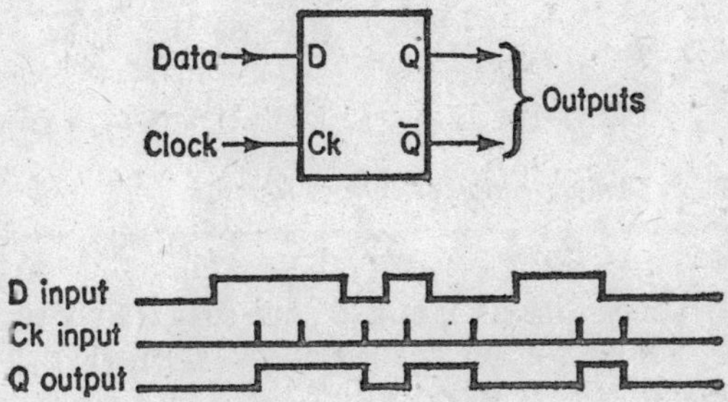

Fig. 2.21 The D-type flip flop.

The clock input acts as a strobe, and each time the clock goes from '0' to '1' the data on D is transferred to the output Q and the complement to $\overline{Q}$. The memory thus freezes the state of D, and is hence often known as a 'latch'.

We can investigate the D type flip flop with the 7474 i.c. connected as shown on Fig. 2.22. The 7474 contains two D types; we will just use one. The clock requires a clean signal, so the de-bounce circuit is used to clean up the contacts of SW1. The 7474 can be used as a normal S-R flip flop by the preset and clear pins (4 and 1 respectively). In our circuit these are disabled by tying them to 5v.

Set SW1 such that CK is at a '0' and SW2 such that D is also as a '0'. (M1 and M2 both out). Pulse CK (i.e. make CK go from '0' to '1' to '0'). The output Q should be at a '0' and $\overline{Q}$ at a '1'.

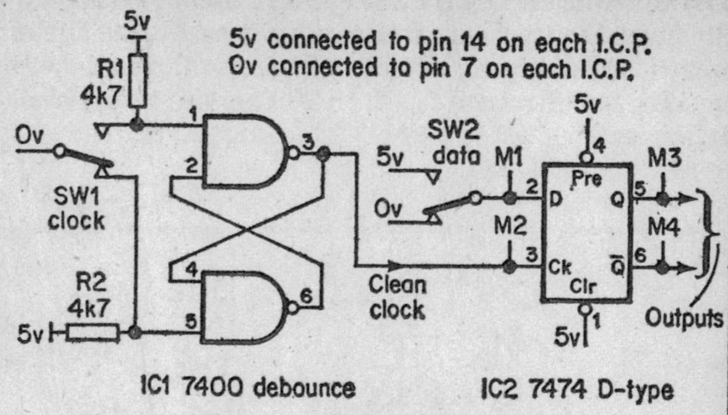

Fig. 2.22 Demonstration of D-type flip flop.

Leave SW1 such that CK is at a '0', but change SW2 such that D is a '1'. Pulse CK again, and the output Q should go to a '1' and $\overline{Q}$ to a '0' to correspond with D.

Try experimenting with D and CK, you should find that changing D without CK has no effect, and changes occur at the instant that CK goes from a '0' to a '1'.

If SW2 is removed, and D is connected to $\overline{Q}$ we get the circuit of Fig. 2.23. It is an interesting intellectual exercise

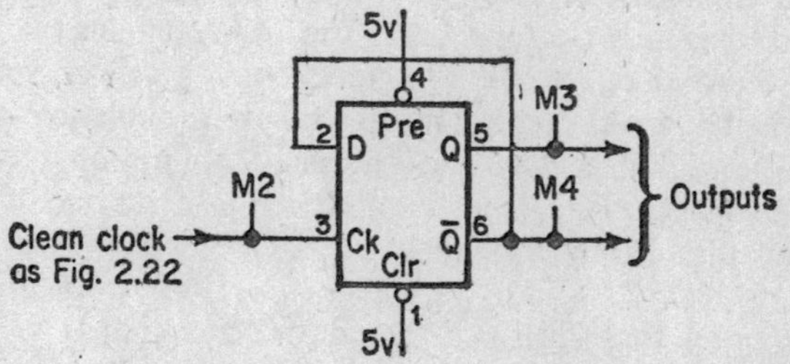

Fig. 2.23 Demonstration of toggling.

to try to predict what will happen as SW1 is pulsed, but it is equally valid to try it and work out why it behaves as it does! The action is known as "toggling" and is a bit like a retractable ball point pen! The toggle is the basis of counter circuits we shall use later.

Our final memory is known as a J-K flip flop. This has three inputs, J, K, and clock and the usual two outputs Q and $\overline{Q}$ as shown on Fig. 2.24. Like the D type flip flop the clock is used to strobe the data on J and K.

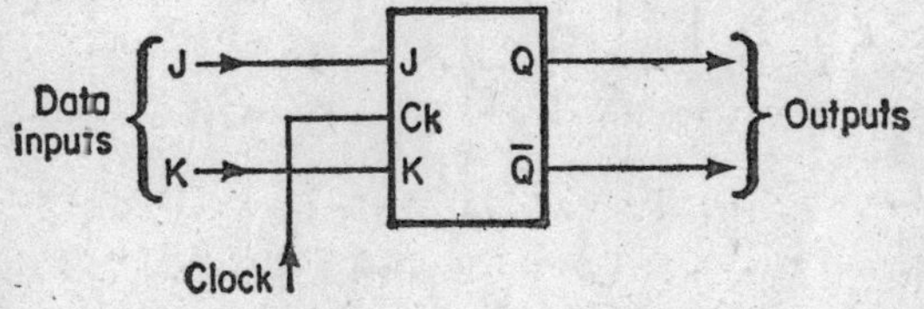

Fig. 2.24 The J–K flip flop.

If J = 1 and K = 0, when CK is strobed we get Q = 1 and $\overline{Q}$ = 0
If J = 0 and K = 1, when CK is strobed we get Q = 0 and $\overline{Q}$ = 1
If J = 0 and K = 0, when CK is strobed Q and $\overline{Q}$ remain in whatever state they are in
If J = 1 and K = 1 when CK is strobed, Q and $\overline{Q}$ toggle.

We can observe the operation of the J-K flip flop with the 7473 i.c. There are two flip flops in the one package, and we use one of them. The flip flop has a clear input (pin 2) which sets Q = 0 and $\overline{Q}$ = 1 when taken to a '0'. In the circuit in Fig. 2.25 the clear input is tied to 5v to keep it out of harms way.

The reader should by now be able to test out the circuit himself, rather than follow a blow by blow description. Points to check out are which edge of the clock signal the circuit operates on, and can J and K be changed without affecting the output.

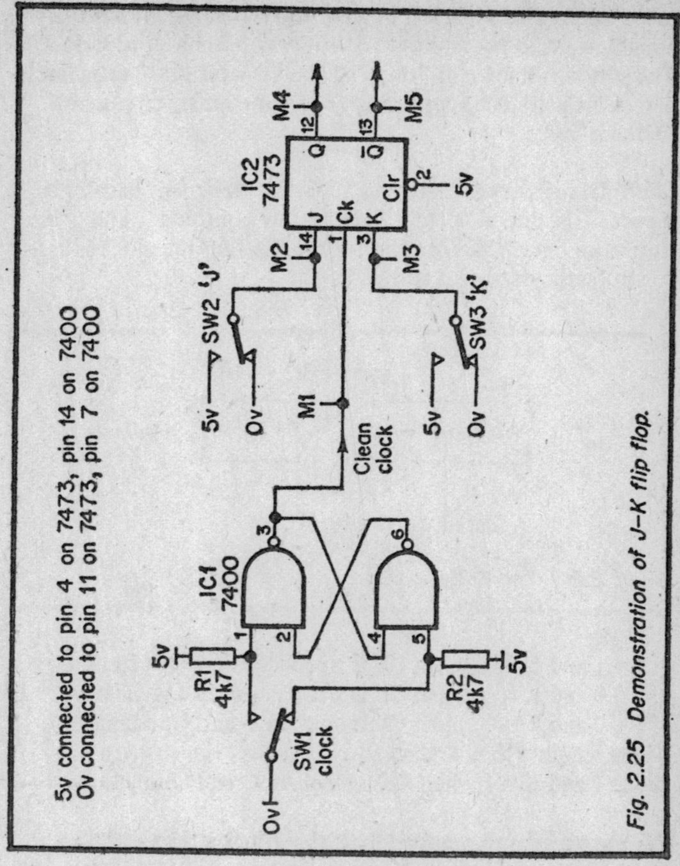

Fig. 2.25 Demonstration of J–K flip flop.

2.4 MONOSTABLES

Logic circuits often need to incorporate some form of a timer. In a gas boiler control, for example, we could say "Open Gas valve, operate igniter for 5 secs, observe if flame present". In a computer input/output unit we could say "Send character to printer, wait for 100mS, check if signal acknowledged." These time delays are usually generated by a special circuit called a monostable.

The simplest form of monostable is provided by the circuit of Fig. 2.26, based on the ubiquitous 555 timer. This device is described in detail in the book "IC 555 Projects" published by Bernard Babani (publishing) Ltd., No. BP44, but its operation is as follows.

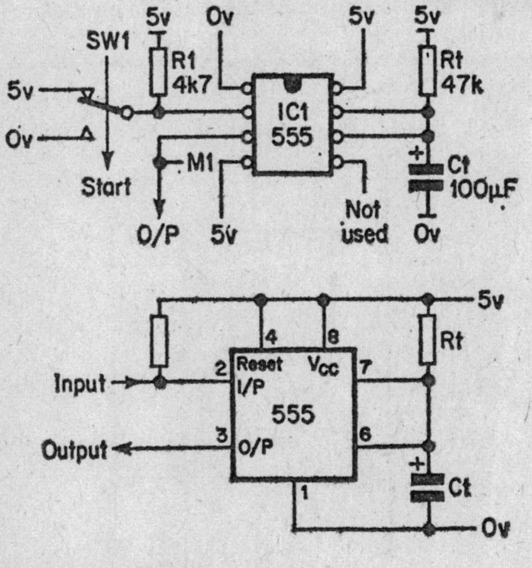

Fig. 2.26 The 555 monostable.

All timers rely on the charging of a capacitor by a resistor, giving a period of about Rt x Ct. The 555 timer is triggered by taking the input, pin 2, to 0v briefly. The output then goes to a '1' and remains there for the timed period, after which it returns to 0v.

The circuit of Fig. 2.26 will give a delay of about 5 secs, allowing its operation to be observed. If a high impedance voltmeter is available the charging of the timer capacitor can be observed. This type of circuit has some shortcomings, the major one of which can be observed by leaving SW1 in the 0v position and observing the output.

This particular shortcoming is overcome by the use of an edge triggered monostable, a typical example of which is the 74121 shown on Fig. 2.27. This can be triggered by a positive edge on pin 5, or a negative edge on pins 3 and 4. To prevent false triggering we feed it from the bounce removing memory described earlier. The tests for the 555 should be repeated, and it should be found that the monostable only fires on the negative edge, and totally ignores the state its inputs are in.

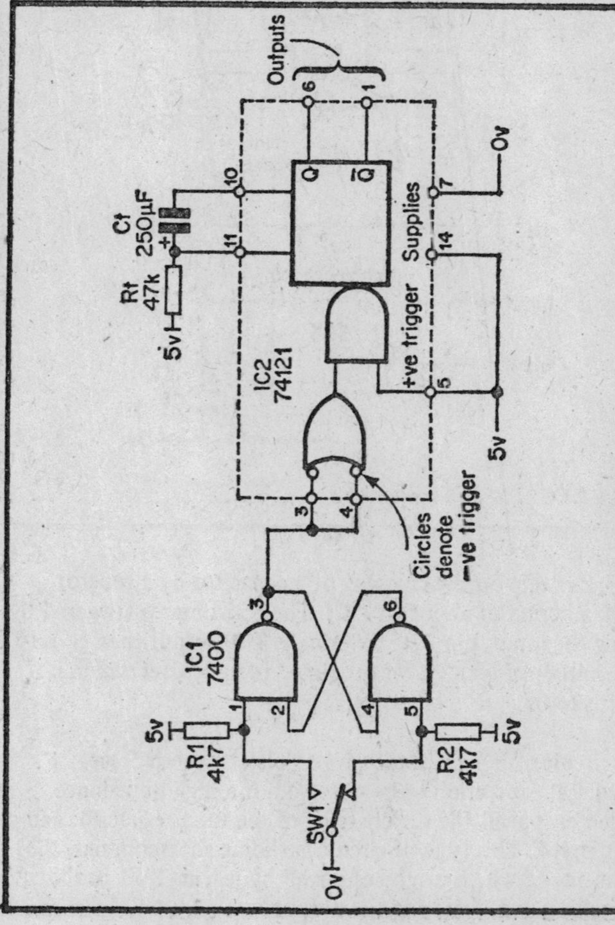

Fig. 2.27 74121 edge-triggered monostable.

Another monostable variant is the re-triggerable 74122 shown on Fig. 2.28. This is triggered by an edge in a similar way to the 74121, but its period restarts for every edge. Again, the input can be positive triggered on pins 3 and 4 or negative triggered on pins 1 and 2. By operating SW1 the behaviour can be observed.

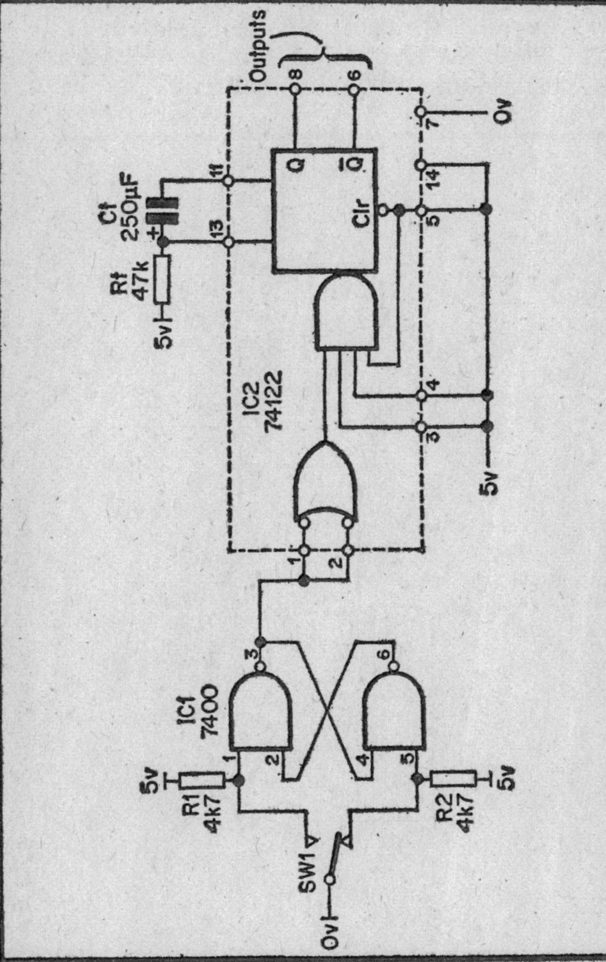

Fig. 2.28 74122 retriggerable monostable.

Re-triggerable monostables are useful for checking the correct operation of equipment. A computer used for industrial control frequently employs a safety check called a "Watchdog Timer". This is an output that the computer makes at regular intervals (usually about 2 times per second). Fig. 2.29 simulates a watchdog timer. IC1 is the computer, simulated by a 555 connected as an oscillator. This kicks the 74122 several times per second. The period of the 74122 is set for about 2 secs, so the Q output will be permanently at a '1' If SW1 is closed, the osciallator will stop and after 2 secs the 74122 will time out, with $\overline{Q}$ giving an alarm.

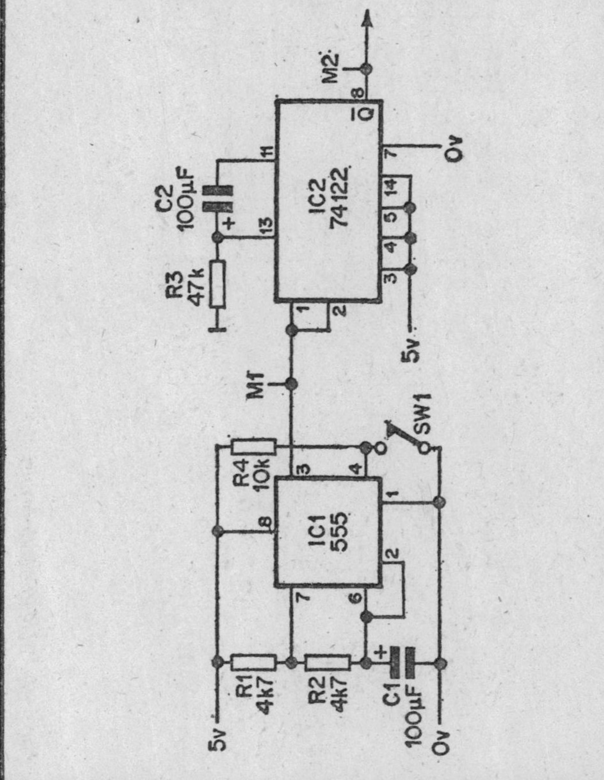

Fig. 2.29 Demonstration of watchdog timer.

Monostables are often used to control a timing sequence. Fig. 2.30 shows a typical timing chain. The switch SW1 fires the 555, which in turn fires the 74121, which in turn fires the 74122. This could obviously be extended if required.

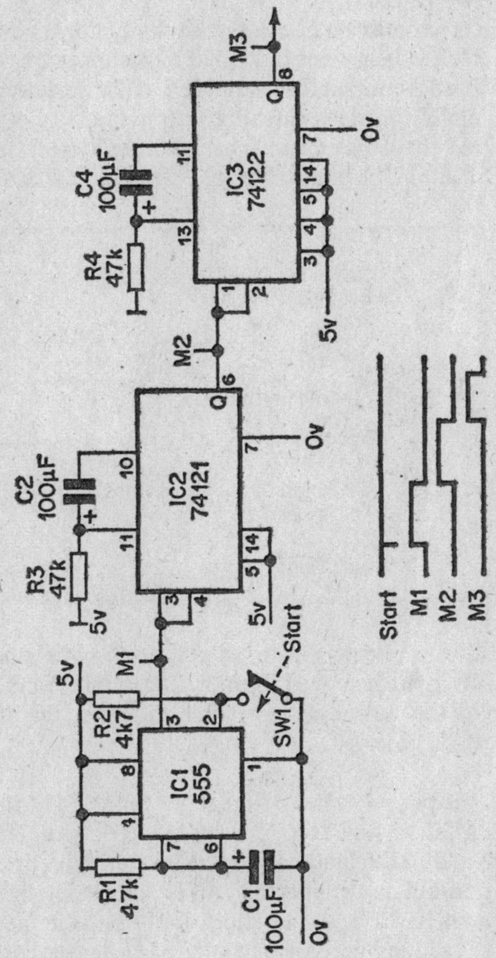

Fig. 2.30 Timing chain experiment.

2.5 SCHMITT TRIGGERS

In control circuits, inputs are often slowly varying, and this is obviously incompatible with the on/off nature of a digital circuit. An i.c.p. called a Schmitt trigger is used to square up a varying signal.

The device is basically an inverter, with the symbol shown on Fig. 2.31. The behaviour is defined by an upper trigger point (UPT) above which the output is a '0', and a lower trigger point (LTP) below which the output is a '1'. Between LTP and UTP the device exhibits backlash (or hysteris to give it its correct name). The backlash gives a clean jitter free output.

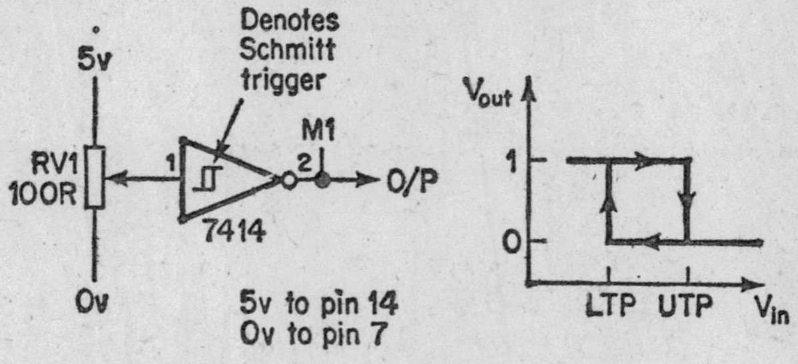

Fig. 2.31 The Schmitt trigger.

The operation can be demonstrated with the 7414 connected as shown. Its input is derived from the potentiometer RV1. The knob on the pot should have some pointer so that its position can be observed.

Start with the pot set such that the input to the 7414 is at 0v. The output, M1, should be at a '1'. Rotate RV1 until M1 changes to a '0'. The change should be crisp with no jitter. Note the position on the pot; this is UTP. Increasing the input voltage should have no further effect. Reduce the input voltage by RV1, and note where the output changes back to a '1'. This is LTP. The changes should again be crisp.

If the circuit is operating correctly, UTP should be higher than LTP, and the difference between the two a measure of the hysteris.

As well as converting slow signals to a digital form, Schmitt triggers are also used in conjucntion with a simple RC filter to remove noise on inputs. Fig. 2.32 shows a typical circuit.

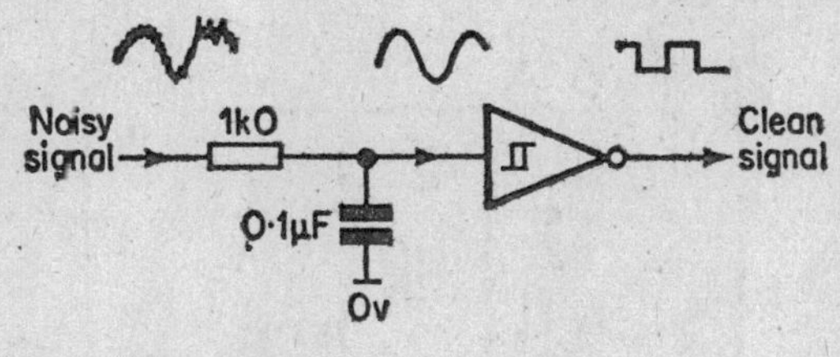

Fig. 2.32 Schmitt trigger filter.

2.6 CONTROL SYSTEMS

The logical elements described so far are the basis of logical control systems not involving arithmetic. As an example of a typical control scheme, Fig. 2.33 shows a possible scheme for controlling a bidirectional motor.

There are three inputs to the system, a forward push button, a reverse push button and a stop push button. A single press on either of the directions button starts the motor, which continues until the stop button or the opposite button is pressed. To avoid motor damage, a delay is introduced such that on reversal of direction, the motor must be stopped for at least 2 seconds before starting in the opposite direction. This is provided by the monostable IC3.

M1 and M2 show "Direction requested". M3 and M4 show the actual drive outputs. M5 shows the inhibit signal from the monostable, and is a '1' for drive allowed.

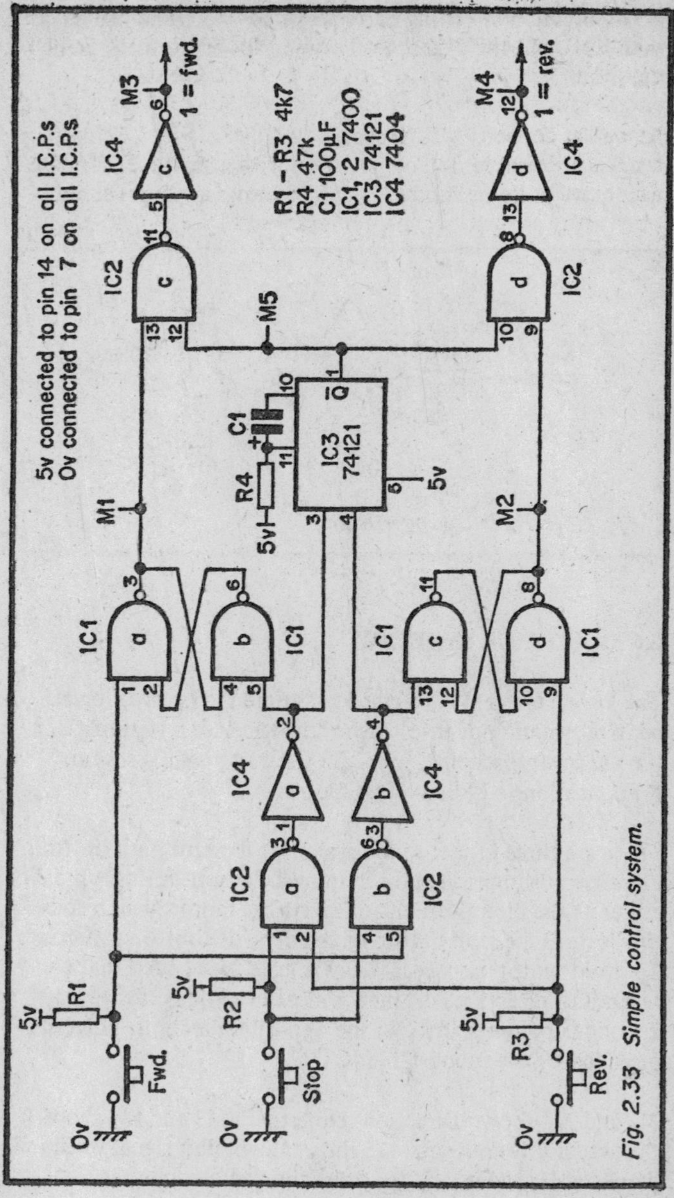

Fig. 2.33 Simple control system.

It should be noted that Fig. 2.33 has some logical shortcomings from a safety point of view, and real control systems would have considerable interlocking to ensure that the circuit fails safe. In Fig. 2.33 the failure of some i.c.p.s. could cause the motor to start of its own accord and be unstoppable short of pulling the fuses. The reader might like to think on the problem of using electronics to control potentially lethal equipment like chemical plants and nuclear reactors.

3. DIGITAL ARITHMETIC

3.1 INTRODUCTION

The second class of digital circuits are those associated with number crunching in one form or another. These can range from a single counter recording the number of baked beans on a conveyer to a large commercial computer.

Arithmetic logic uses the '1's and '0's to represent numbers, and manipulate them as required. We must first decide how we can represent numbers so the logic can recognise them.

3.2 NUMBER REPRESENTATION AND THE BINARY SYSTEM

We count in tens, purely because we have ten fingers. The number :–

4057

thus represents:–

	4 x 10 x 10 x 10 =	4000
plus	0 x 10 x 10 =	0
plus	5 x 10 =	50
plus	7 =	7

It would be very nice to have logical systems operating in units, tens, and hundreds, and it would be quite feasible, technically, to do this. We could, for example, represent each decade by 10 lines (labelled 0 to 9). One line at a time would go to a '1' to represent the number.

A scheme similar to this was used in some early computers, and is still found in some pocket calculators. Such a scheme is, however, very wasteful of electronics and more elegant schemes have been devised.

A few moments experimentation with a pad and pencil will

show that any number can be obtained by summing combinations of multiples of two (1, 2, 4, 8, 16, 32, 64, 128, 256, 512, 1024, etc.).

For example:—

$$5 = 4 + 1$$
$$15 = 8 + 4 + 2 + 1$$
$$27 = 16 + 8 + 2 + 1$$
$$108 = 64 + 32 + 8 + 4$$

If we represent a number internally by the equivalent multiples of two we will produce the simplest possible electronic circuits. For example, all numbers from 0 to 1023 can be represented by 10 wires (and you can count from 0 to 1023 on your 10 fingers for that matter).

This system is known as the Binary System. It allows any number to be represented as a combination of '1's and '0's representing the presence (or absence) of a power of two. It is usual to write the least significant power of two to the right, and the numbers 0 to 15 are given below:—

	Multiples of two			
	8	4	2	1
0	0	0	0	0
1	0	0	0	1
2	0	0	1	0
3	0	0	1	1
4	0	1	0	0
5	0	1	0	1
6	0	1	1	0
7	0	1	1	1
8	1	0	0	0
9	1	0	0	1
10	1	0	1	0
11	1	0	1	1
12	1	1	0	0

13	1	1	0	1
14	1	1	1	0
15	1	1	1	1

The sequence of digital numbers on the right is known as the binary representation of the numbers on the left. The sequence can obviously be continued indefinitely. Adding a column for 16 for example, would allow representation of numbers up to 31.

Each binary digit (i.e. a '1' or a '0') is called a bit. Four bits can thus represent any number from 0 to 15.

Working in binary is all very well for the electronics, but is impossibly laborious for us humans with 10 fingers. At the input and output of the electronics we need some circuits to convert between binary and decimal. These are known as encoders and decoders.

3.3 ENCODER

An encoder converts from decimal to binary, a typical unit being the 74147 shown on Fig. 3.1. This has 10 decimal inputs (0 to 9) and 4 binary outputs (8, 4, 2, 1 labelled D, C, B, A respectively). The inputs are selected by a '0', and the outputs are in complement form. The inputs are therefore selected by taking the required input to 0v by SW1, and the outputs are inverted by the 7404 before being monitored by M1 – M4. Note that the input representing zero is inferred.

Ideally a rotary decade switch should be used for SW1, but a radio wave change switch or a simple line of pins and a flying lead could be used at considerably less cost.

As SW1 is rotated to select various numbers, M1 – M4 should indicate the corresponding binary number. After tests, do not dismantle this circuit as it is the start of other circuits to be described later.

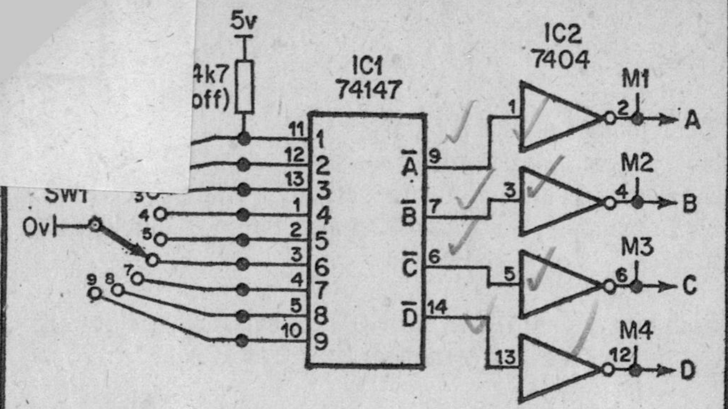

Note:
IC1 is 16-pin DIL.
4k7 pull-up resistors required on SW1 outputs,
No connection is needed to SW1 position '0'.
All inputs high implies '0' input.
5v connected to pin 16 on IC1 & pin 14 on IC2.
0v connected to pin 8 on IC1 & pin 7 on IC2.

Fig. 3.1 Decimal to binary encoder.

3.4 DECODERS

In general, decoders convert binary to decimal. A typical circuit is the 7442 decoder shown on Fig. 3.2. This takes binary in on A, B, C, D and gives the decimal equivalent of 0 to 9. The outputs go to a '0' when selected.

The circuit uses the encoder from section 3.3 to produce a binary number. This is connected to the decoder which should produce the number selected on SW1.

If required, all 10 outputs could be monitored, but this would be somewhat of an overkill. A simple logic probe with a flying lead is suggested to monitor the outputs. This needs to be preceeded by an inverter as the outputs are in complement form (remember!).

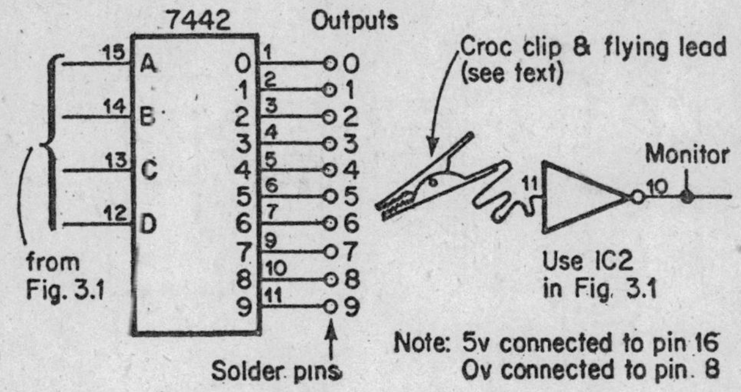

Fig. 3.2 Binary to decimal decoder.

The circuit of Fig. 3.2 can be modified to produce a recognisable number by means of a seven segment display. A seven segment display consists of seven LEDs arranged as shown on Fig. 3.3. By turning on selected segments any number from 0 to 9 can be displayed.

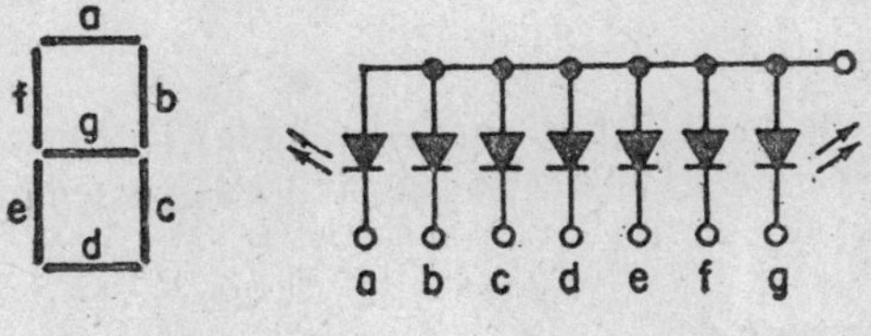

Fig. 3.3 The seven-segment display.

Special binary to seven segment decoders are available which can drive a seven segment display directly. A typical device is that the 7447 shown on Fig. 3.4 connected into the circuit of Fig. 3.2. The seven resistors R1 – R7 limit the current through the LEDs to a safe value. Pin 3 on the 7447 is a lamp test input. If it is taken to 0v all the seven segments are illuminated.

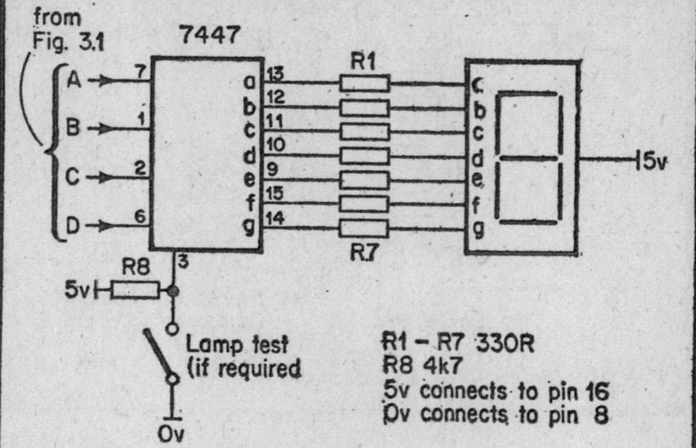

Fig. 3.4 Seven–segment decoder.

With Fig. 3.4, a decimal number can be selected on SW1. Its binary equivalent will be displayed on M1 – M4. The decoded decimal output can be observed on the seven segment display or monitored on the output of the 7447 with the flying lead probe.

The seven segment display and its encoder will be used in several experiments below, and should be left assembled.

3.5 COUNTERS

In many applications some form of counter is required. In section 2.3 we described toggle flip flops constructed from D type and J-K flip flops. These are the basis of most counters.

Fig. 3.5 shows two 7474 dual D type i.c.p.s. connected to form a four bit counter. The coupling of $\overline{Q}$ back to D makes each stage toggle. The clock input on the first stage is derived from a bounce removing flip flop for reasons described earlier. Switch SW2 resets the counter to zero.

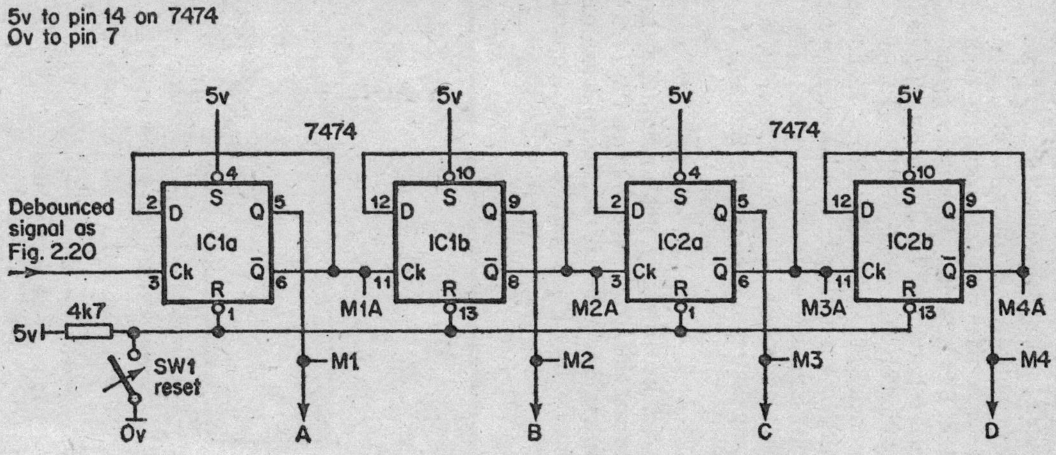

Fig. 3.5 4–bit counter.

There are several experiments that can be tried with Fig. 3.5, apart from the simple demonstration of a binary counter. Try connecting the seven segment decoder and display from Fig. 3.4 to the Q outputs, (A to M1, B to M2 etc.). Try connecting the seven segment decoder and display to the $\overline{Q}$ outputs (A to M1A, B to M2A etc.). Does this suggest how we can make a counter count down? Try dispensing with the bounce removing flip flop and drive the first clock input direct from the switch SW1. With most switches, the bounce will make the switch count unreliably. If the seven segment decoder and display is used, observe what happens to the display as the counter goes beyond a count of nine. Since the display can only show 0 to 9 the decoder gets a bit confused!

Because counters are used so widely, it is not surprising that counter i.c.p.s are available. A typical example is the 7493 counter shown on Fig. 3.6. As before the counter is fed from a bounce removing flip flop. Pins 2 and 3 are a reset, operating on a '1' level.

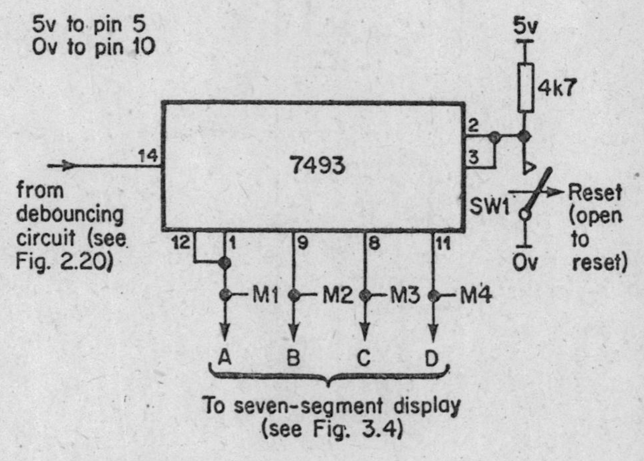

Fig. 3.6 4-bit binary counter I.C.P.

Counters are available to count to any base, and Fig.
shows a 7490 counter to base 10. This counts from 0
then resets itself. If its outputs are connected to the s
segment display and decoder, the previously observed
displays will not occur. Two resets are available on this counter; pins 2 and 3 reset to a zero state for a '1', and pins 6 and 7 reset to a 9 for a '1'. Note that the pinning of Fig. 3.6.and 3.7 are identical, allowing a quick and easy change between the two counters.

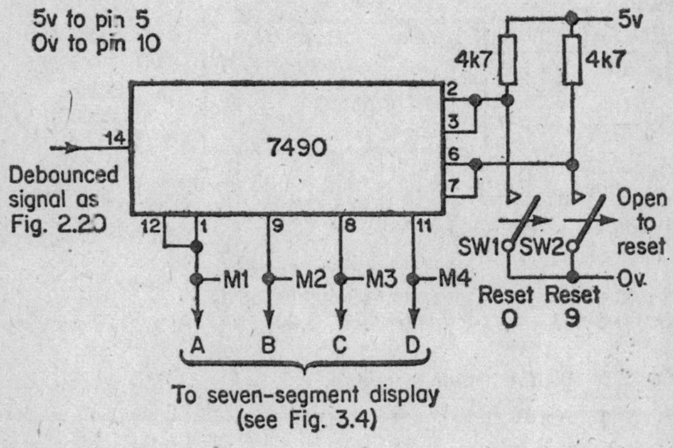

Fig. 3.7 Decade counter I.C.P.

In the description of Fig. 3.5 we saw that a counter can be made to count up or down. A bi-directional counter whose direction can be changed at will can be made from the 74190 shown in Fig. 3.8. This has a count input from a normal bounce removing memory, and the usual 4 bit output. In addition it has a single line (pin 5) which determines the direction of count. This can be controlled by SW1. It should be found that the counter will count up or down as determined by SW1. The 74190 has a facility that we do not use (mainly because of the large number of switches it would require to demonstrate). Pin 11 acts as a reset pin, but it does necessarily reset to zero. The user can present a 4 bit number to pins 15, 1, 10, 9 and the counter will go to that value when pin 11 is strobed. This facility is very useful for, say, counting the number of items to go in a batch. The number required is loaded into the counter, which counts down for each item. When it reaches zero the batch is complete.

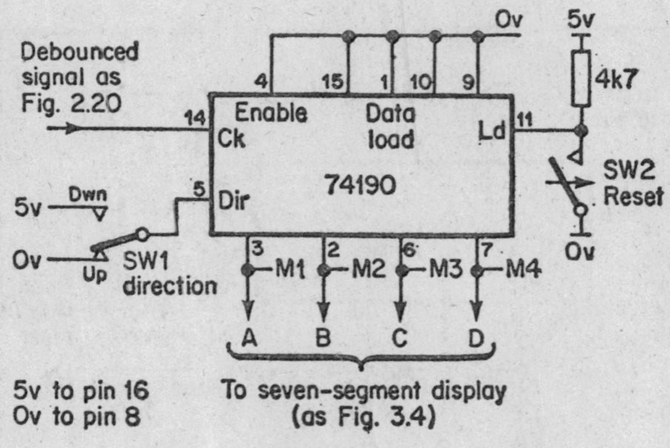

Fig. 3.8 Bi-directional counter.

3.6 ADDERS

Before describing how a binary adder works, we must first consider what we do when we add two numbers. Consider the simple decimal addition.

$$\begin{array}{r} 457 \\ +714 \\ \hline 1171 \\ \hline \end{array}$$

Doing a sum like this we put the numbers in columns with each column representing (from the right) units, tens, hundreds, thousands etc. As you perform the addition, your mind goes something like "seven plus four is eleven, one down and one to carry, five plus one is six plus the carry is seven" and so on.

The addition of two three digit numbers thus really comprises the addition of three pairs of single numbers along with any carry from the previous stage, and each pair can be represented as:—

$$\begin{array}{l} \quad A \\ +B \\ \underline{+ \text{carry from right}} \\ = \text{SUM OUT} \\ \text{and carry to left} \end{array}$$

At each stage we have three inputs (A, B, and carry in) and two outputs (sum and carry out).

Binary addition is similar, but simpler. Binary addition is based on the simple rule:—

Decimal	Binary
0 + 0 = 0	0 + 0 = 0
0 + 1 = 1	0 + 1 = 1
1 + 1 = 2	1 + 1 = 10

A single digit binary adder can be represented by Fig. 3.9.

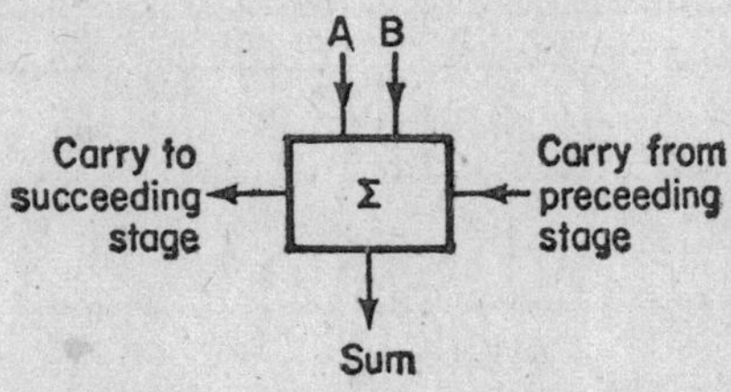

Fig. 3.9 Block diagram of single-bit adder.

This has out three inputs and two outputs described above. A quick thought should show that the following relationship is needed between the three inputs and the three outputs:

INPUTS			OUTPUTS	
A	B	Cin	Cout	SUM
0	0	0	0	0
0	0	1	0	1
0	1	0	0	1
0	1	1	1	0
1	0	0	0	1
1	0	1	1	0
1	1	0	1	0
1	1	1	1	1

Given a single adder block, an adder can be produced to any described number of bits. Fig. 3.10 shows a 4 bit adder. Note that a 5 bit answer is given, in the same way that two 3 decade decimal numbers can be added to give a 4 decade result.

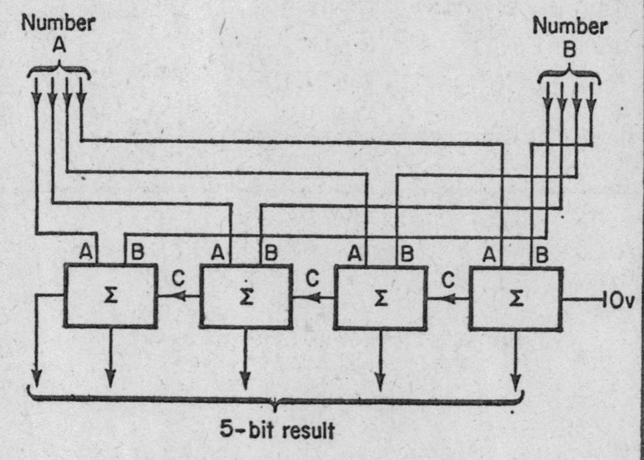

Fig. 3.10 Block diagram of 4-bit adder.

There are many ways of generating the adder logic tabl[illegible] common method being the use of two half adder circuits a[illegible] shown on Fig. 3.11. The half adder simply adds two bits, ignoring the carry in. Its logic table is thus:–

A	B	Cout	Sum
0	0	0	0
0	1	0	1
1	0	0	1
1	1	1	0

The sum produced by a half adder is then added to the carry in another half adder to produce the final sum and carry. A practical version is shown on Fig. 3.11, which utilises the capabilities of the NAND gate to give both the AND and OR functions.

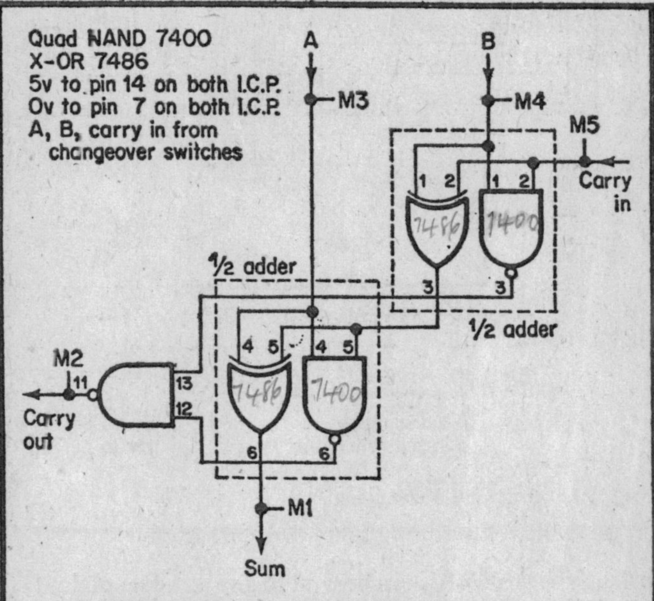

Fig. 3.11 Practical adder using 2 half adders.

cted by now, adder i.c.p.s are readily
g. 3.12 shows a four bit adder based on the
W2 select a number in the range 0 – 9.
ted to four bit numbers as described in
7483 adds these to give a 5 bit result which
n the monitor LEDs (or on a seven segment
display if SW1 and SW2 are set such that the resulting sum does not exceed decimal ten). Note that the first carry in is connected to 0v.

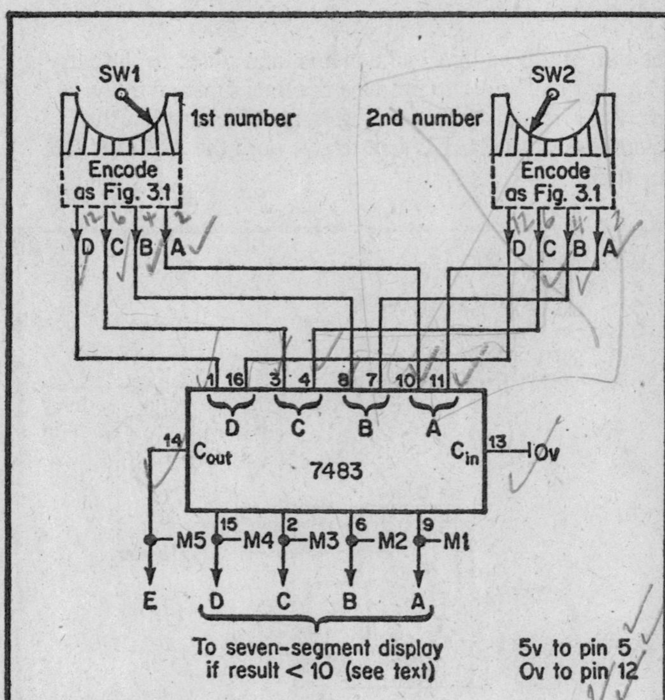

Fig. 3.12 Practical 4-bit adder.

Obviously several 7483s can be used to give an adder of any desired length. With large adders, a speed problem is encountered. Consider the sum:–

```
 1111111111111111
 0000000000000001
10000000000000000
```

The extreme right hand addition produces a carry which has to propagate through each successive stage to finally produce the most significant '1'. This is known as a "Ripple through Carry" and is a major speed restriction. Complex adders employ a "look ahead" technique to predict carries, and hence speed up the operation. The reader will therefore see adder i.c.p.s described as "ripple through" or "look ahead" carry.

3.7 SUBTRACTION

Subtraction can be achieved by simple addition. Consider the sum below:–

```
 023
 994
1017
```

If we ignore the "thousand" column, the answer is 17. The number 994 thus looks like minus 6. Another example :–

```
 251
 827
1078
```

Again, ignoring the "thousand" column, the answer is 78. The number 827 thus looks like minus 173.

A three digit decimal negative number is formed by subtraction from one thousand. Minus 6 is thus given by 1000 – 6 = 994.

Negative binary numbers are formed in a similar manner. Consider the binary sum:–

	0110	(binary 6)
	1100	
	1 0010	(binary 2)

The number 1100 thus represents minus 4. Another example:–

	0111	(binary 7)
	1011	
	1 0100	(binary 4)

The number 1101 thus represents minus 3.

It is actually very easy to produce a negative number. Take the number to the required number of bits, complement it, and then add '1'.

e.g.

0110	binary 6
1001	complemented
1010	add 1

1010 thus represents minus 6. Another example:–

0011	binary 3
1100	complemented
1101	add 1

1101 thus represents minus 3.

Note that the most significant bit represents the sign, and is '1' for a negative number and '0' for a positive number. A four bit number can thus represent a number in the range 0 to +15 OR –8 to +7 BUT NOT both ranges at the same time. Similar arguments apply to any number of bits. 8 bits, for example, can represent a number from 0 to 255 OR –128 to +127.

Fig. 3.13 shows Fig. 3.12 modified to be an adder/subtractor.

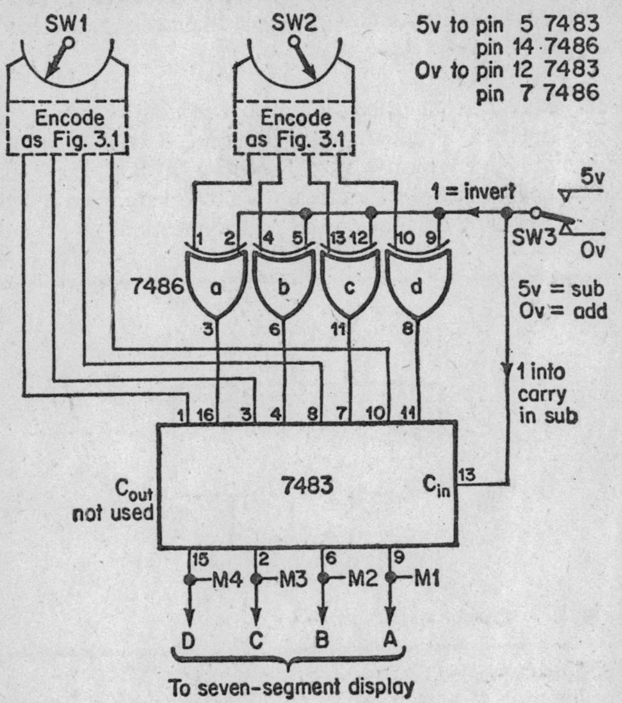

Fig. 3.13 Adder/subtractor.

The mode is selected by SW3. The quad enclusive or gate is used to invert the 4 bits from SW2 when subtraction is selected, and a '1' is added by injecting '1' into the least significant carry in on the 7483. Note that in the subtraction mode SW1 must be larger than SW2, and both must be in the range 0 to 7.

3.8 SHIFT REGISTERS

It might be expected that the section following addition and subtraction might be devoted to multiplication and division.

In practice, multiplication and division are rather rare, but before we can deal with them we must first investigate circuits known as shift registers.

A shift register is a multibit store whose contents can be moved one bit at a time to left or right. Fig. 3.14 shows the connections to a typical 4 bit shift register. A, B, C, D are the four inputs (A least significant) and Qa to Qd are the outputs. Data is loaded by a strobe on the load connection.

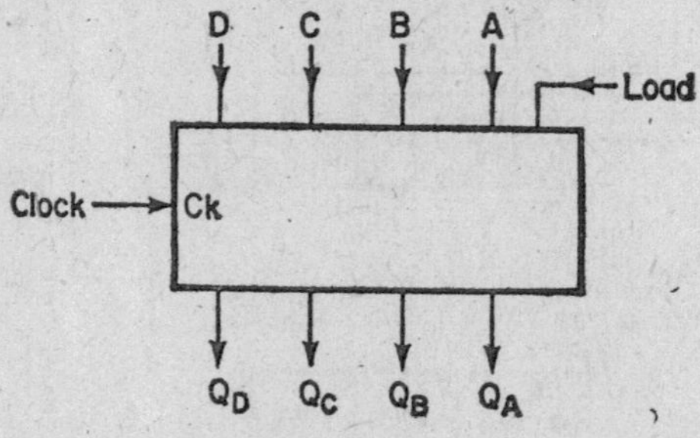

Fig. 3.14 Typical shift register.

The direction of movement is determined by the Up/Down line, being a '1' for, say, up and '0' for down. Each time a pulse is applied to the clock input, the data moves one bit in the desired direction. In most shift registers, bits spilling off the end are lost and '0's are fed in at the other end.

Suppose we have loaded 1101 into the shift register, and we have selected shift up. After successive clock pulses we will have:—

	D	C	B	A
start	1	1	0	1
clock pulse 1	1	0	1	0
clock pulse 2	0	1	0	0
clock pulse 3	1	0	0	0
clock pulse 4	0	0	0	0

A four bit shift register constructed from D types is shown on Fig. 3.15. The Q output from one stage is connected to the D input on the next stage. Every time the clock line is strobed, the data will move one bit to the right. The shift register shifts down therefore.

Data is loaded by first resetting the shift register with SW5, then setting the required data on SW1 – SW4. As the

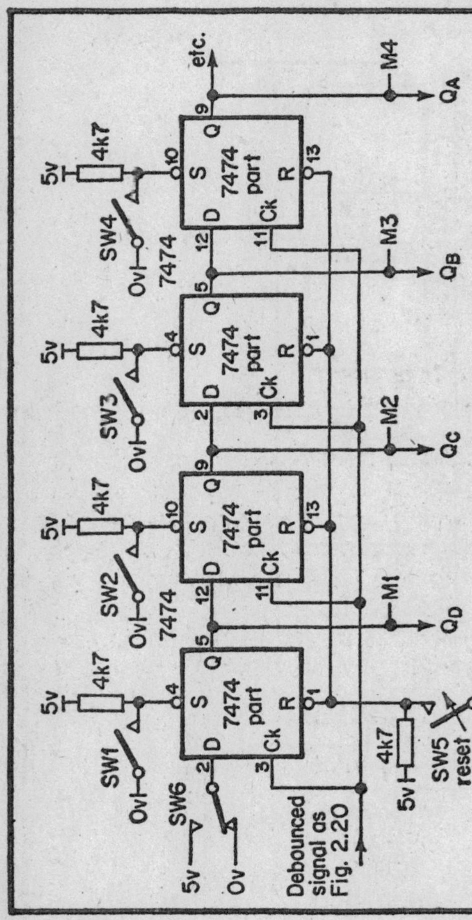

Operation: Reset with SW5,
Load data on SW1 – SW4,
Debounced signal clocks shift register,
Data shifted into Q_D from SW6.

5v to pin 14
0v to pin 7

Fig. 3.15 Four-bit shift register.

buffered switch operates, the data will move one bit down for each switch pulse, and can be observed on M1 – M4. SW6 sets data shifted into the most significant end.

Shift registers can also be made with J-K flip flops, and Fig. 3.16 shows a four bit shift register. The Q and Q outputs are connected to the J-K inputs of the next stage. When the clock line is strobed, data is transferred.

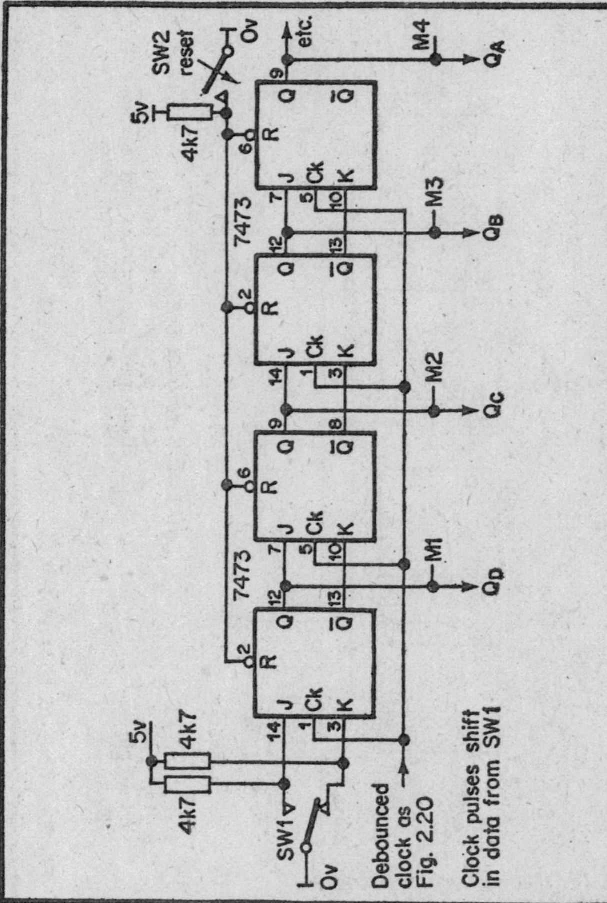

Fig. 3.16 Four-bit shift register with J – K flip flops.

There is obviously no real difference between unidirectional shift up and shift down registers, the connections are the same and the direction is purely a matter of convention as to which end is which! Bidirectional shift registers where the direction can be changed are more complex, requiring gates to select whether the stage input is connected to succeeding or preceding stage.

Where a shift register is required, it is usual to employ a shift register i.c.p., typical of which is the 74194 shown on Fig. 3.17. This is a 4 bit bi-directional shift register, with ABCD the four parallel inputs, Qa – Qd the corresponding outputs and the usual clock. In addition there are two control lines, S0, S1, which determine the operational mode as below:–

S1	S0	Operation
0	0	Inhibited
0	1	Shift right
1	0	Shift left
1	1	Parallel load

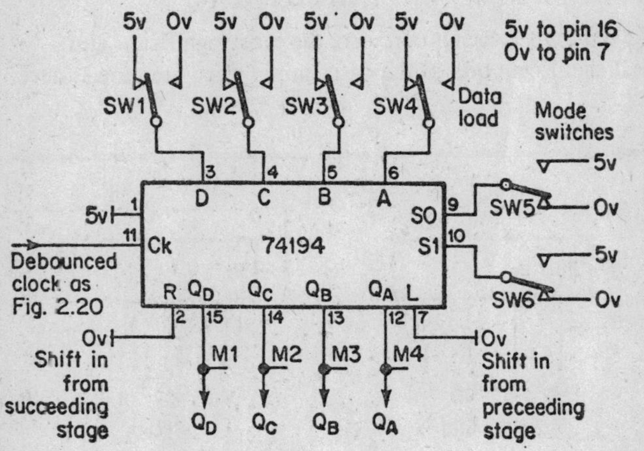

Fig. 3.17 Bi-directional shift register.

The operation of the shift register can be observed by means of the switches SW1 – SW6, and observing the outputs monitored on M1 – M4.

Shift registers can be built to any length, and the shift register i.c.p.s can be cascaded to any desired length. To facilitate this, a serial right input and a serial left input are provided. These provide the link between stages by connection to the corresponding outputs on the preceding and succeeding stages.

On Fig. 3.17 these serial inputs (pins 2 and 7) are connected to 0v. If they are connected to switches the operation of the serial inputs can be observed.

Variations on the basic shift register are shown on Fig. 3.18. An arithmetic shift register maintains the top sign bit on shift down keeping the sign correct. The operation is thus:–

Negative number	Positive number
1 1 0 0 1 0 1 1	0 1 0 0 1 0 1 1
1 1 1 0 0 1 0 1	0 0 1 0 0 1 0 1
1 1 1 1 0 0 1 0	0 0 0 1 0 0 1 0

A cyclic shift register connects the most significant and least significant bits so the data simply circulates and is never lost.

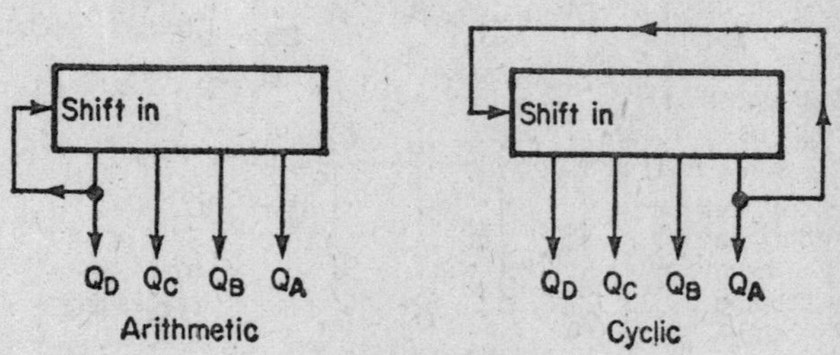

Fig. 3.18 Shift register variations.

3.9 MULTIPLICATION AND DIVISION

Multiplication and division are not common operations, so only the outline principles will be given. Let us first consider a decimal multiplication:

```
   413
 x  25
 -----
  8260
  2065
 -----
 10325
```

We perform the multiplication a digit at a time, and add the resulting part results. Note in particular that the result has more digits than either of the numbers multiplied. In general, the multiplication of two two digit numbers can result in a four digit result. The same applies to binary numbers, and 8 bits are needed to express the results of multiplying two 4 bit numbers.

The operation of binary multiplication is similar to decimal multiplication, except the rules are simpler. The basic single digit multiplication rules are:–

$0 \times 0 = 0$

$0 \times 1 = 0$

$1 \times 0 = 0$

$1 \times 1 = 1$

This is obviously an AND function.

A binary multiplication thus looks something like:–

```
  1 0 1 1
x   1 0 1
---------
    | | └──────→ 1011 x 1        1 0 1 1
    | └────────→ 1011 x 0      0 0 0 0 ·
    └──────────→ 1011 x 1    1 0 1 1 · ·
                             -----------
                             1 1 0 1 1 1
```

The basis of a multiplier is shown on Fig. 3.19. As can be seen it is fairly complex, and hence is shown only in block diagram form. The two numbers to be multiplied, A and B, are 8 bits long. These are loaded into two registers: A into the least significant 8 bits of a 16 bit shift register, B into a simple store. Associated with B is same logic to select one bit of B at a time. The results register, R, is initially cleared.

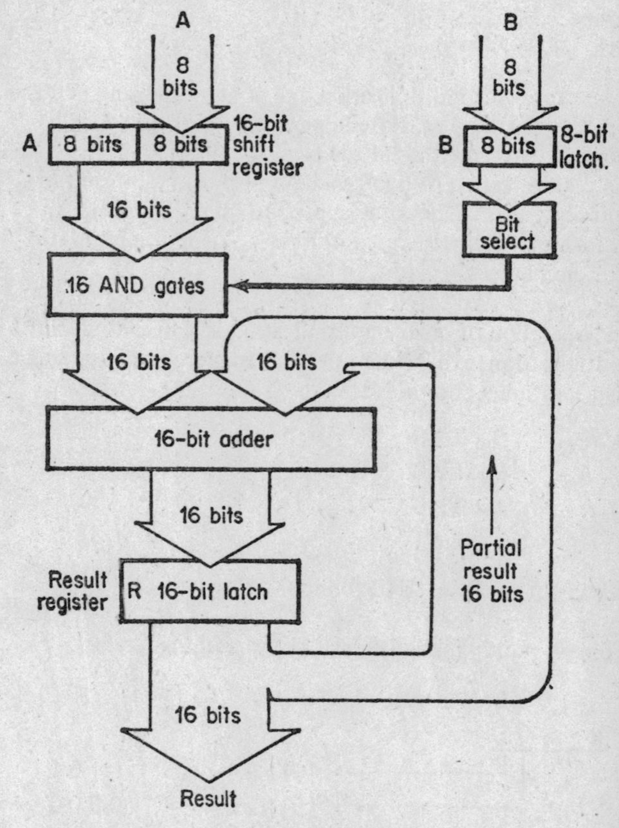

Fig. 3.19 Block diagram of 8-bit multiplier.

The operation takes several clock pulses. A is gated with the least significant bit of B and added to the results register to produce a new partial result. A is then shifted one bit to the left, gated with the next bit of B and added again to produce a new partial result. The sequence is repeated for all 8 bits, when the result is held in the results register. Obviously the operation is time consuming and expensive.

Fast multipliers are available which produce the result in one operation. Basically these consist of a large read only memory on which the result is "looked up". These are expensive, but are used in computers with hardware multiplication.

Division is accomplished in a similar manner, except shifts and subtraction are required. Division circuits are very rare.

In general, with the costs of LSI falling month by month, it is usually more cost effective to use a microprocessor where multiplication and division are required. Although very few computers have hardware multiply and divide, it is very easy to perform the data manipulation required in Fig. 3.19 by computer program.

4. COMPUTER ARCHITECTURE

4.1 INTRODUCTION

In the preceding sections we have covered the logical elements that are used to make a computer. We can now see how these pieces fit together to form a machine. Of necessity the description of how a computer works will be brief, and for a fuller description the reader is referred to the author's book "A Microprocessor Primer" also published by Bernard Babani (publishing) Ltd., Book No. BP72.

A computer can be considered similar to a simple clerical job. We would provide a clerk with a desk, an in tray, an out tray, a pad of paper for doodling part results on, a set of files, a calculator and a list of instructions to follow.

The block diagram of a computer shown on Fig. 4.1 compares directly with our clerical job. The data comes into the system via the connections labelled "Data in", and processed data through the connection labelled "Data out". These connections, known as Ports in the jargon, will go to printers, V.D.U.s, tape readers etc.

The instructions for the computer to follow are held in the store, along with data to be processed. The store can be considered as a large array of pigeonholes. Each pigeonhole has a unique address and data can be stored in each pigeonhole. Associated with the store is an address buffer which is used to hold the address of the location being accessed, and a data buffer which is used to hold the data being loaded into, or read from, the store.

The next part of the computer is the ALU. The letters stand for Arithmetic and Logic Unit, and this is equivalent to the clerks scribbling pad and calculator. The ALU contains an arithmetic unit that can perform addition, subtraction, shifts etc. and several general purpose registers (four in the illustration). Each register can hold one "number" and are used for temporary storage in the middle of calculations.

The control ties the computer together. It decides which instruction is to be obeyed next, reads it from the store, decodes it and decides what action to take. Having obeyed the instruction it moves onto the next instruction. This selection of instructions is done by the instruction counter. In addition, the control produces the necessary timing signals to ensure events happen at the right time. The control can thus be considered similar to the clerk himself.

Finally we have the backing store. This is bulk storage (usually magnetic tape or disc) used to store large amounts of data that can be accessed relatively slowly.

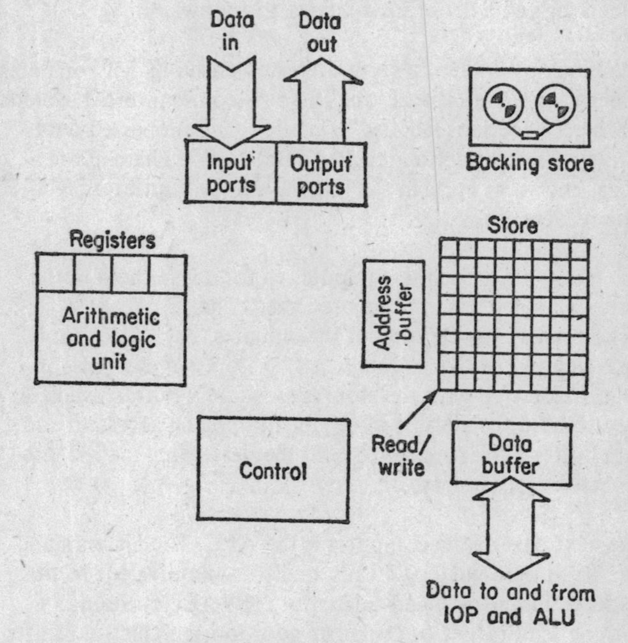

Fig. 4.1 Block diagram of typical computer.

4.2 THE STORE

Instructions and data for the computer are held in the store in Fig. 4.1. This consists of pigeonholes, each pigeonhole having a unique address and being capable of holding one binary number.

Computer stores normally have a considerable number of pigeonholes, 4K (4096) being the smallest useful size and 64K (65536) being typical of a large system. Each location can hold either 8 bits (called 1 byte), 16 bits or 32 bits depending on the computer.

We can build a model of a computer store with the 7489 RAM i.c.p. This is a small store with 16 locations, each location capable of holding one 4 bit number.

The store has four address lines, which allows us to address 0 to 15 (i.e. 16 locations), four data in lines, four data out lines, and a read/write line. In block diagram form, the store can be represented by Fig. 4.2.

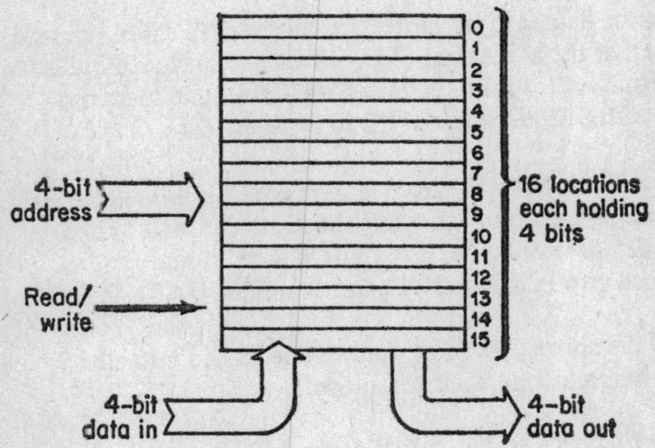

Fig. 4.2 The 7489 RAM store.

To write information into the store, the address is set on the address lines and the data on the data lines, with the read/write line in the "read" state. The read/write line is then strobed, and the data passes into the selected store location.

To read information from the store, the address is set on the address lines, and the read/write line is left in the "read" state. The data appears on the data out lines.

To demonstrate this operation we need the circuit of Fig. 4.3. IC1, 2 and 3 are quad latches used to buffer the inputs and outputs. Each i.c.p. contains four D type flip-flops, which are loaded when the clock input goes to a '1'.

The address is set on SW1 to SW4, and strobed into IC1 by SW10. The address can then be read on M1 to M4. Data to be loaded is set on SW5 to SW8, and strobed into IC2 by SW9. It can then be read on M5 – M8. The write operation is controlled by SW12, data being written when pin 3 is a '0'. To prevent inadvertant "writes", ideally SW12 should be made a spring return push button. Data read from the store appears on pins 5, 7, 9, 11 where it is strobed into IC3 by SW11, and can be observed by M9 – M12.

To write data into the store, first ensure SW12 is in the read state. Set the address on SW1 – SW4 and load into IC1 with SW10. Next set the data onto SW5 – SW9 and load into IC2 with SW9. Operate SW12 to store the data.

To read data from the store, ensure SW12 is in the read state. Set the address on SW1 – SW4 and load into IC1 as before. The data is now available on pins 5, 7, 9, 11 and can be strobed into IC3 with SW11 and examined by M9 – M12.

With the above operation, data can be loaded into all 16 locations and read back as required.

Referring back to Fig. 4.1, IC4, the 7489, corresponds to the store, and IC1 to the address buffer. IC2 and IC3 correspond to the data buffer. We have used separate buffers for data being written into the store and read from the store. Computers, in general, use a common buffer for both and select the direction of data flow with gates. This would have complicated our simple store unnecessarily.

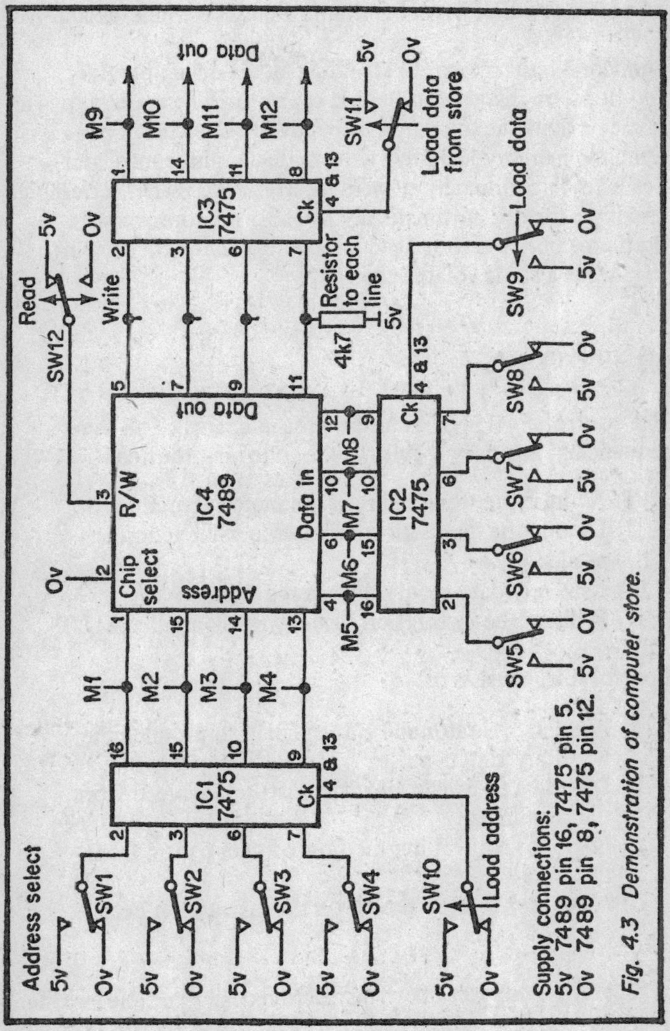

Fig. 4.3 Demonstration of computer store.

Computer stores can be classified as volatile or non volatile, and static or dynamic. A non volatile store keeps its contents when the power is removed, a volatile memory looses its contents. In general, non volatile memories are based on magnetic cores and all semiconductor memories are protected by batteries where loss of contents would be embarrassing.

Semiconductor memories are either based on simple S-R flip flops, or charge storage on a capacitor. These are known as static or dynamic memories respectively. The charge in a dynamic memory leaks away over a few milliseconds, and needs to be continually re-written. This is known as refreshing, and is performed automatically by most microprocessors. Static memories do not need refreshing. The 7489 used in Fig. 4.3 is a static volatile memory.

4.3 CONTROL

The control portion of a computer is in charge of all the sequencing. Basically it follows the following routine:

i) Address the store and read the next instruction
ii) Decode the instruction and decide what action is needed
iii) Read any data required from the store
iv) Perform the instruction (usually involving the ALU)

Control thus consists of:–

a) A clock generator and timing chain to produce the necessary timing pulses
b) Decoders to decide what the instructions read from the store mean
c) Logic for controlling the flow of data to and from the store
d) A counter to keep record on the instruction being obeyed.

In general a computer obeys instructions one at a time in order. It then obeys instruction 1, then instruction 2, then instruction 3 and so on.

In "A Microprocessor Primer" the operation of conditional jumps and unconditional jumps are described which allow the computer to leap out of sequence, but in general it does proceed one instruction at a time. The instruction counter can therefore be a simple binary counter, stepped each time the computer completes an instruction.

An instruction usually defines two things; firstly the operation to be performed, (add, subtract, store, fetch etc.); secondly, the store location involved (e.g. fetch the contents of store location 1234).

Having read an instruction the control splits it into its functional and address portions. The function part is decoded to determine the operation required, and the address portion is used to address the store.

Data within a computer flows along highways, and data flow can be from any register to any other register (e.g. memory buffer to register A, or instruction counter to address buffer). Transfer of data from place to place is achieved by the control operating gates as required by the instruction being obeyed.

The fundamental component used in constructing a highway is the Tristate gate. This is similar to a normal logical gate, with the addition of a control input. Fig. 4.4 shows a tristate buffer. With the control input enabled, the gate behaves as a normal buffer, with a '1' in producing a '1' out. With the control input disabled the output goes to a high impedance

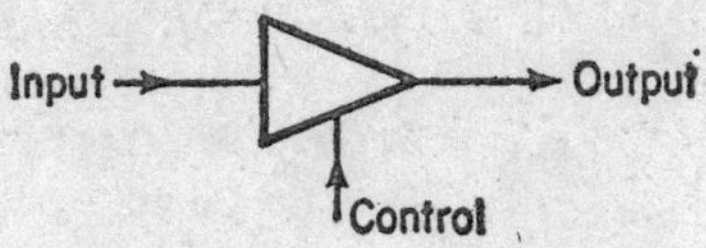

Fig. 4.4 The tristate gate.

state (i.e. floating). Several tristates gates can thus be connected to a single line, and data placed onto the line from several places as shown on Fig. 4.5.

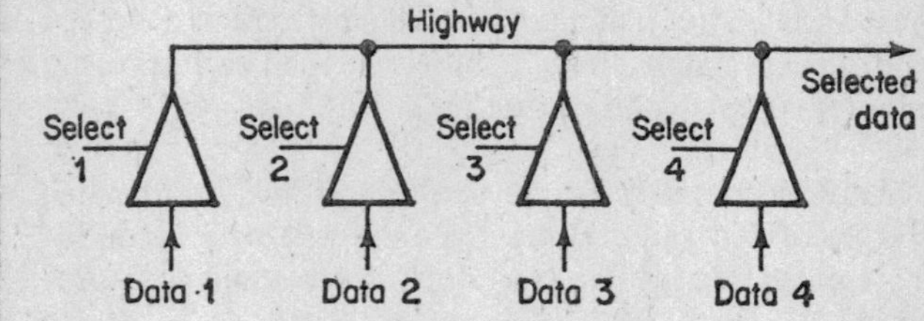

Fig. 4.5 Tristate gates for data selection.

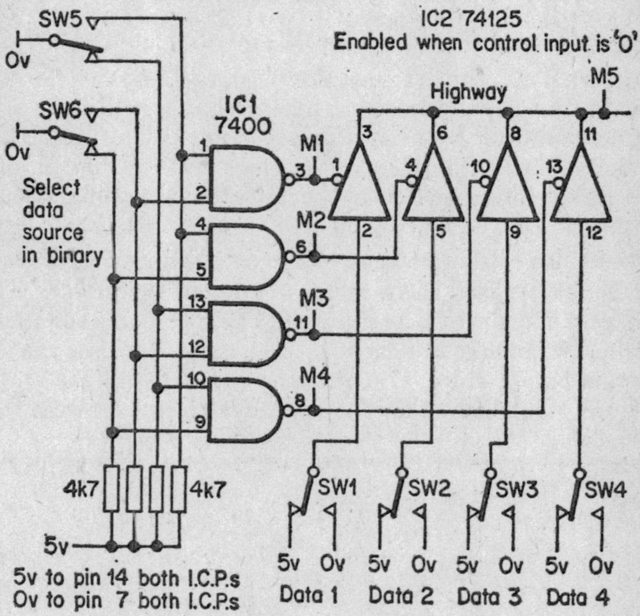

Fig. 4.6 Demonstration of tristate gates.

The operation of the tristate gate can be demonstrated with Fig. 4.6 IC2 is a quad tristate buffer, with the control input being a '0' to enable the gates. SW1 to SW4 represent 4 different data sources and M5 the reception point. The line linking the outputs of IC2 thus represents one line of a data highway.

Selection of the data source is done by SW5 and 6 and IC1. IC1 decodes the binary selection on SW5 and SW6 to enable one, and only one, gate in IC2. This approach guards against double selection. Monitor points M1 to M4 show the selected gate.

It should be found that SW5 and SW6 allow data flow from one selected switch in SW1 to 4 onto the highway which can be monitored by M5.

The control portion of a computer thus operates the necessary gates at the correct time to allow data to flow as required.

4.4 ARITHMETIC AND LOGIC UNIT

The arithmetic unit performs the operations such as Add, And, Subtract, Shift etc. required by the program instruction. Normally the ALU will comprise a logical block to perform the necessary operations and several general purpose registers. A register is a collection of flip flops, each capable of holding one number.

The use of G.P. registers speeds up calculations as they can be used as stores for partial results without accessing the main store. The programmer thus uses them as a "scribbling pad".

A block diagram of the ALU of Fig. 4.1 is shown on Fig. 4.7. The four registers, A, B, C, D and the arithmetic unit are connected to the highway (which goes onto the store and the input/output). The control sends signals to conduct the operation. Suppose we want to add the contents of register A and B and store the result in store location 1234. The control

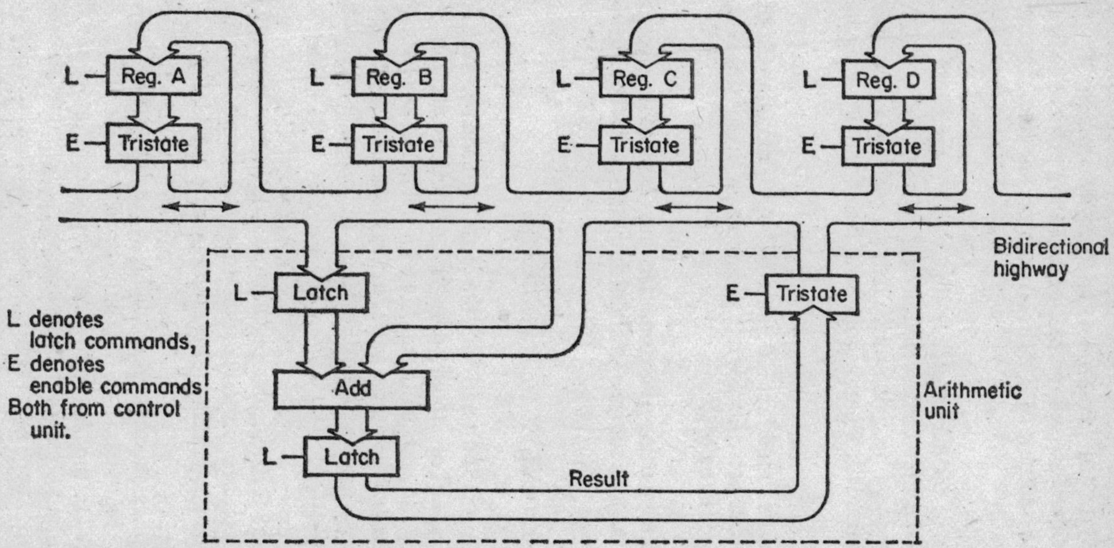

Fig. 4.7 Simplified block diagram of ALU.

would send the following sequence:–

a) Register A, put contents on highway
b) Arithmetic Unit, read in highway
c) Register B put contents on highway
d) Arithmetic Unit add highway and number previously read in.
e) Address buffer : 1234
f) Arithmetic unit, put result on highway
g) Memory buffer, read in highway
h) Store write

The arithmetic unit itself will be similar to the 7483 we experimented with in section 3.6, with additional logic to perform the AND, OR functions required by programs and latches to store numbers coming from the highway.

The register themselves will be similar to the 74194 shift register we used in section 3.8 to allow storage of numbers and shifts to take place. The arithmetic unit and the registers will be connected onto the highway by the tristate gates described earlier.

4.5 A MODEL COMPUTER

In this section we describe a model computer that demonstrates data flow inside a computer. The control section of the computer is provided by the reader, who will operate the necessary switches to route the data as required. This simplifies the design considerably as the instruction decode logic and the timing chain are the most complex (but not the most difficult to understand) parts of the machine. In operating the model the reader will come to understand the design requirements of the control section of the machine.

The diagram of the machine is shown on Fig. 4.8. The computer has the 16 locations store from section 4.2 (IC17), two registers, IC13 and IC4 and a 7483 based arithmetic unit all connected via tristate gates to a bi-directional highway.

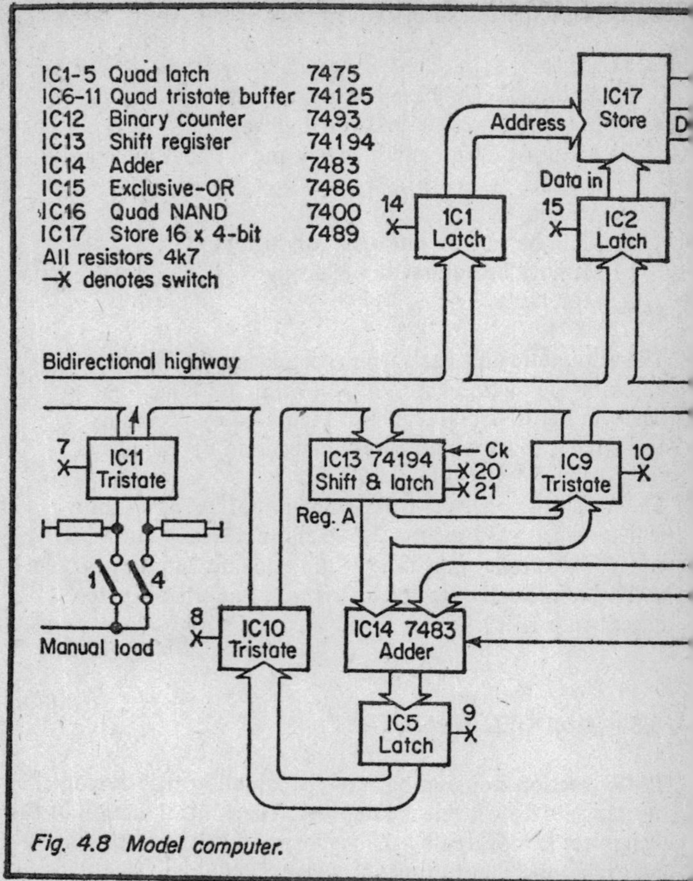

Fig. 4.8 Model computer.

Where a number is required to be held, the 7475 quad latch is used (e.g. IC1).

The highway is four bits wide, and it is suggested that ribbon cable is used. To prevent noise problems, the total length should be no longer than about 30 cms, and there should be no spurs.

Monitoring is left to the readers financial restraints, but at

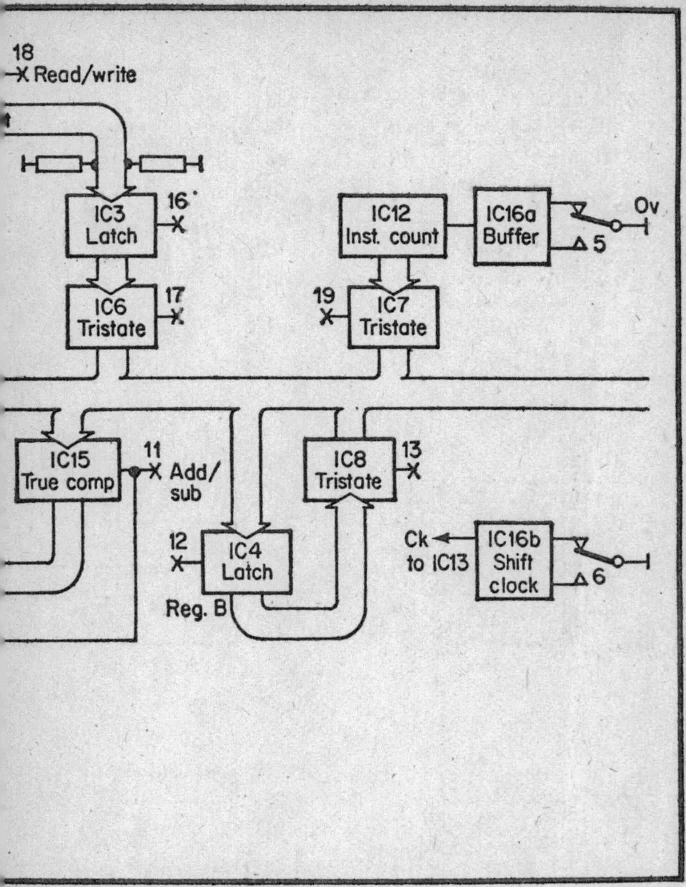

least IC13 output, IC3 output, IC1 output and the highway itself should be monitored (3 off 7406 and 16 off LEDs).

Fig. 4.8 is drawn diagramatically and pin connections are not shown as this would complicate the diagram unnecessarily. Fig. 4.9 shows the pinning of all the i.c.p.s used in this book, and if you do not feel competent to build the circuit from this information the de-bugging is probably beyond you anyway!

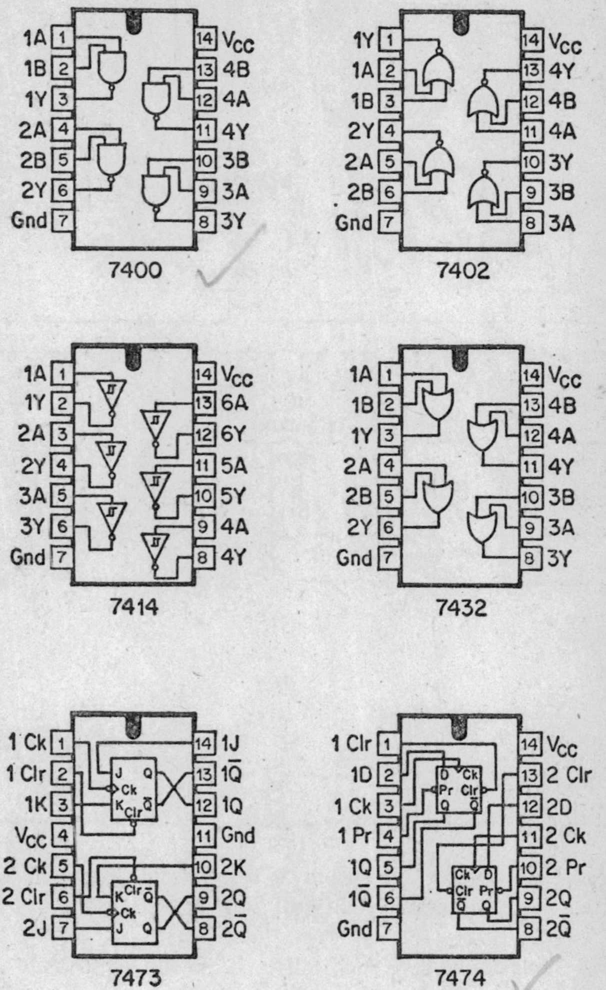

Fig. 4.9 TTL circuits used in this book.

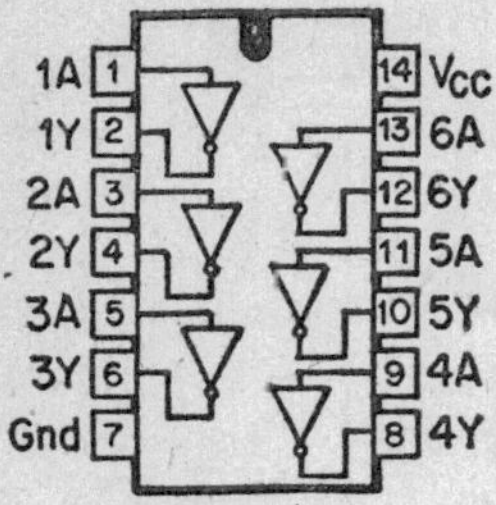

7404 & 7406

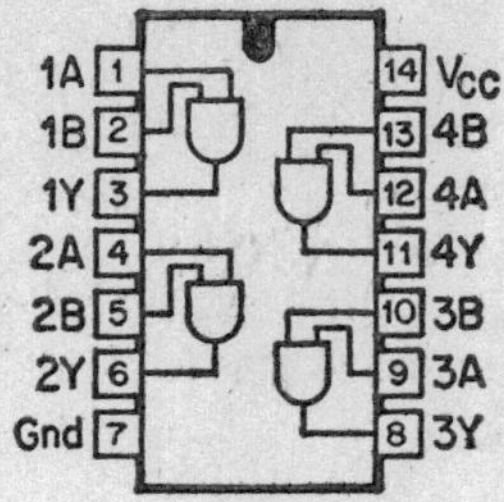

7408

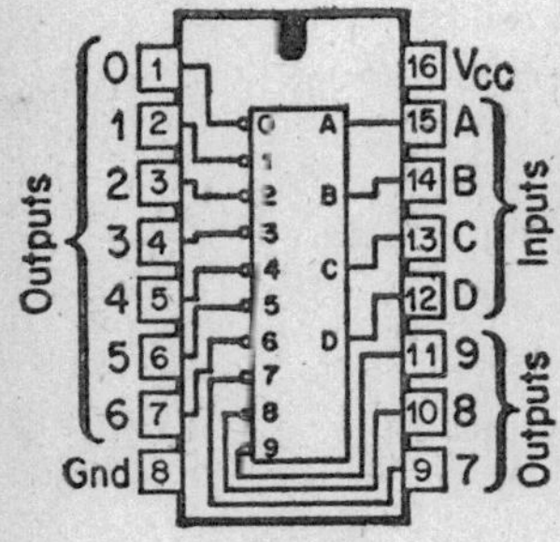

7442

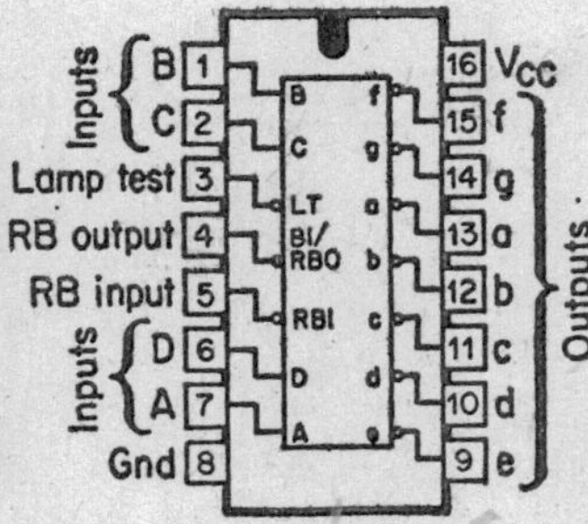

7447

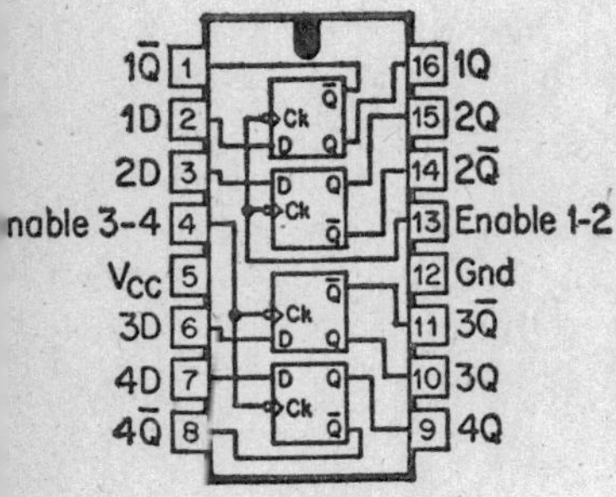

7475

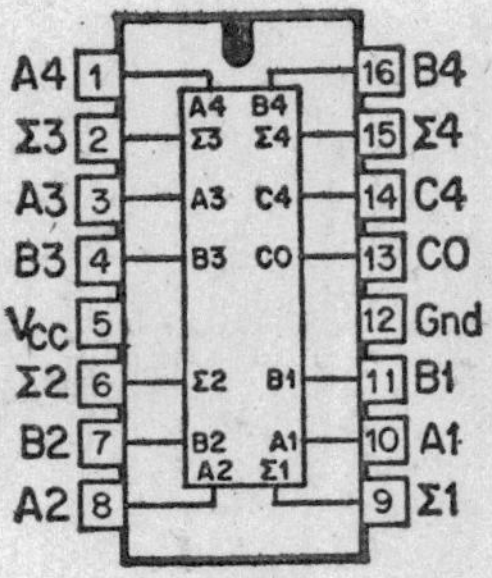

7483

(cont.)

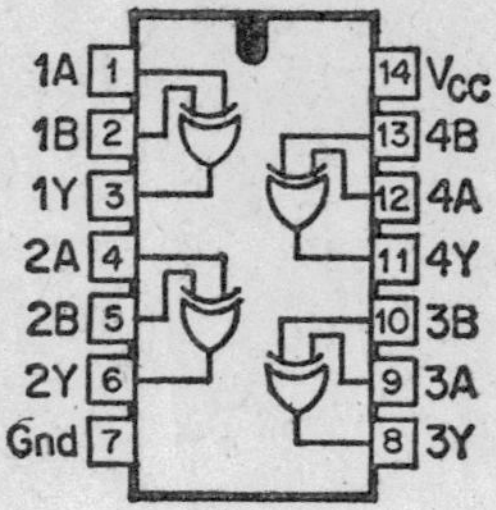

7486

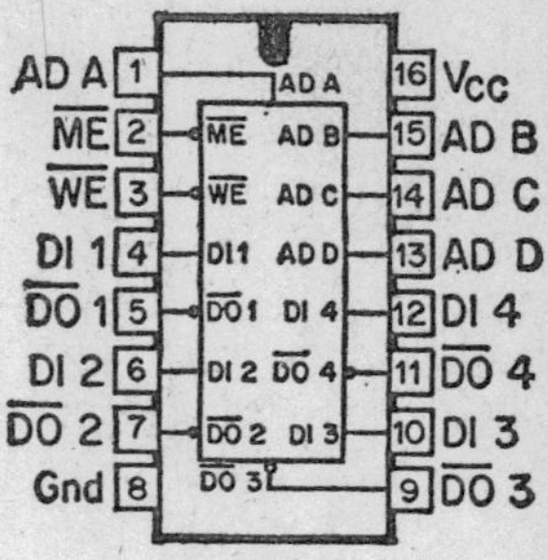

7489

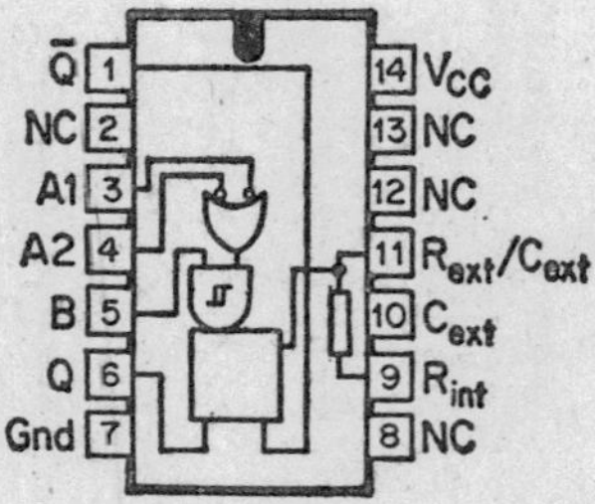

74121

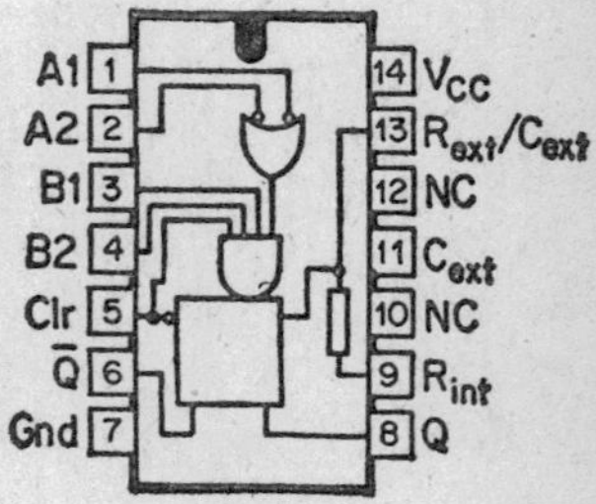

74122

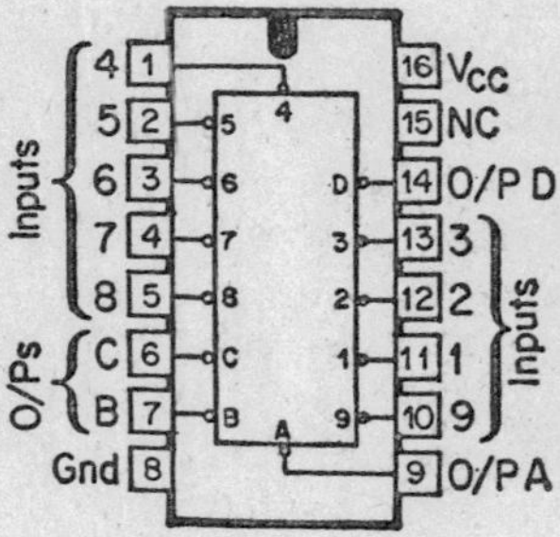

74147

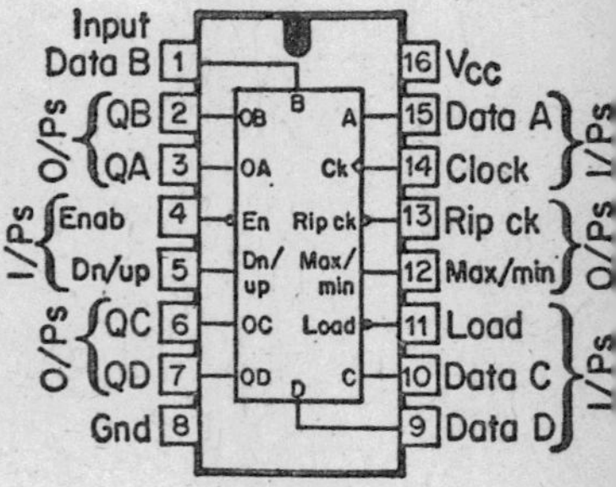

74190

(Fig. 4.9 cont.)

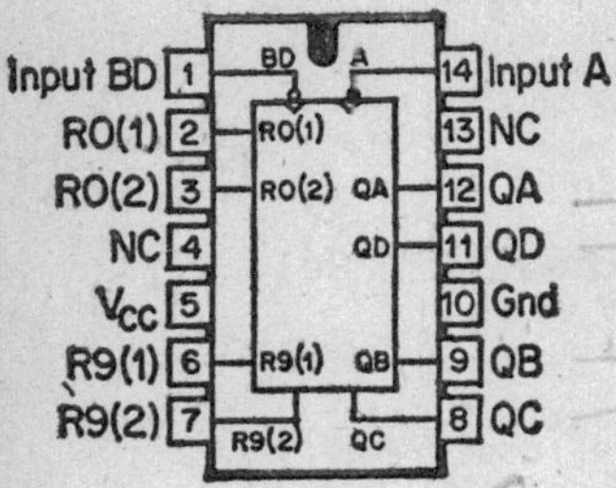

7490

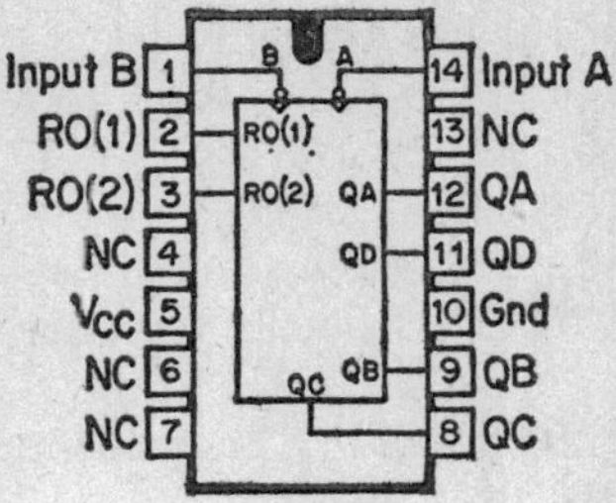

7493

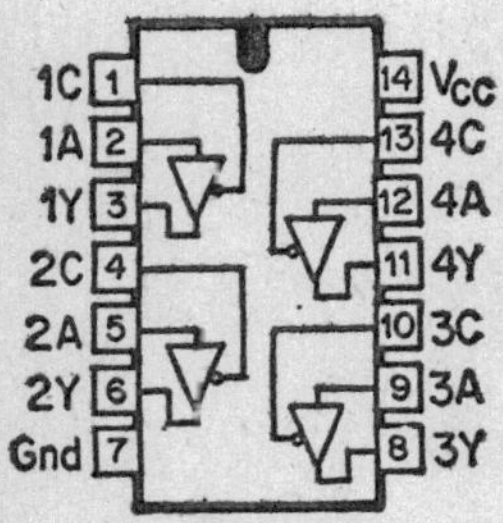

74125

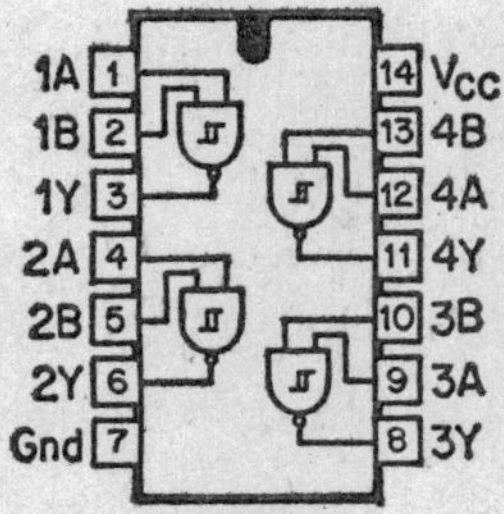

74132

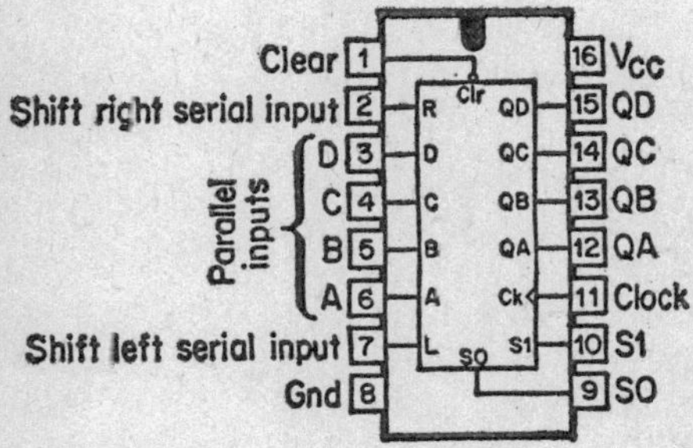

74194

Definition of A – D may vary on data sheets

On Fig. 4.8:

IC1, 2, 3, 6, 17 corresponds to the store
IC13, 9 to register A
IC10, 5, 14, 15 to the arithmetic unit
IC4, 8 to register B
IC11 allows manual inputs
IC12, 7 allow sequential stepping through store locations
IC16 is two bounce removing flip flops

The circuit can best be understood by running through a few examples.

Example 1: Loading data from manual switches.

a) Set address on SW1 – SW4
b) Enable IC11 (SW7)
c) Strobe latch IC1 (SW14)
d) Set data on SW1– SW4
e) Enable IC11 (SW7)
f) Strobe latch IC2 (SW15) Data is now ready
g) Strobe write line (SW18)

Data is now in selected address.

Example 2: Adding data stored in locations 8 and 9, and placing result in location 10. As these are sequential locations we will use the step facility on IC12.

a) Step IC2 to '8' with SW5
b) Enable IC7 (SW19)
c) Strobe latch IC1 (SW14) Address now loaded
d) Strobe latch IC3 (SW16) Data now read
e) Enable IC6 (SW17)
f) Strobe latch IC13 (SW20 and 21)
Data is now in register A
g) Step IC12 to '9' with SW5
h) Enable IC7 (SW19)
i) Strobe latch IC1 (SW14) Address now loaded
j) Strobe latch IC3 (SW16) Data now read
k) Enable IC6 (SW17)
l) Set SW11 to Add Output of adder is now result

m) Strobe latch IC5 (SW9)
n) Step IC12 to '10'
o) Enable IC7 (SW19)
p) Strobe latch IC1 (SW14) Address loaded
q) Enable IC10 (SW8)
r) Strobe latch IC2 (SW15) Data in memory buffer
s) Strobe write line (SW18)

Result is now stored as required.

Finally we will take data from register B, shift it up two places and return it to register B.

Example 3:

a) Enable IC8 (SW13)
b) Strobe latch IC13 (SW20 and 21)
   Data is now in register A
c) Set SW20 and SW21 for shift up
d) Press SW6 twice Register A shifts up twice
e) Enable IC9
f) Strobe latch IC4

These examples indicate the techniques used in moving data around, and simulates the operation of a real machine with the reader taking the part of the control logic. Using the logic the machine can shift up, shift down, add, subtract, multiply and (with some dexterity on behalf of the user) divide.

4.6 THE MICROPROCESSOR

Contrary to popular belief a microprocessor is not a computer. It is, in fact, the control and ALU of a computer and needs the addition of external i.c.p.s such as a store, clock, i/o logic before it can be made into a machine which we will call a microcomputer.

A typical microprocessor is the Z - 80, whose internal elements are shown on Fig. 4.10. The Z - 80 works with 8 bit data and a 16 bit address. The Z - 80 thus speaks to the outside world on two highways; an 8 bit data highway and a 16 bit address highway.

Internally the Z - 80 has 16 8 bit registers which are interconnected via an internal bus. In addition there are several 16 bit registers used for addressing the store.

The instruction register is used to hold the current instruction which is decoded and implemented by the control logic. The ALU operates as described above.

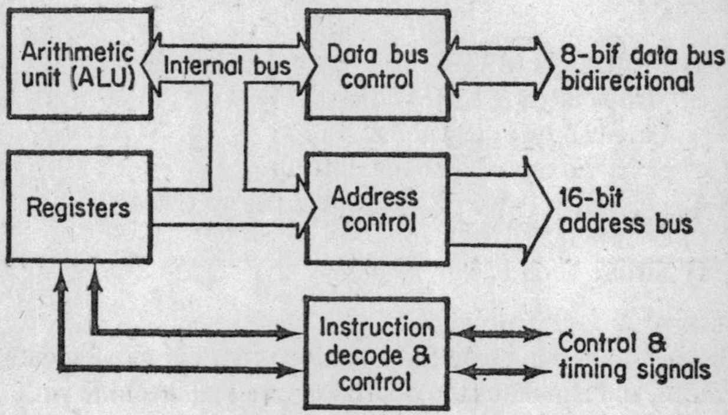

Fig. 4.10 Block diagram of Z-80 C.P.U.

A Z - 80 connected as part of a microcomputer is shown on Fig. 4.11, with the necessary external components shown. This is probably the smallest useful computer possible. The read only memory contains the system operating program, and as its name implies this memory cannot have its contents altered by the computer.

4.7 INPUTS AND OUTPUTS

To be useful a computer needs to communicate with the outside world. This communication will take place in either

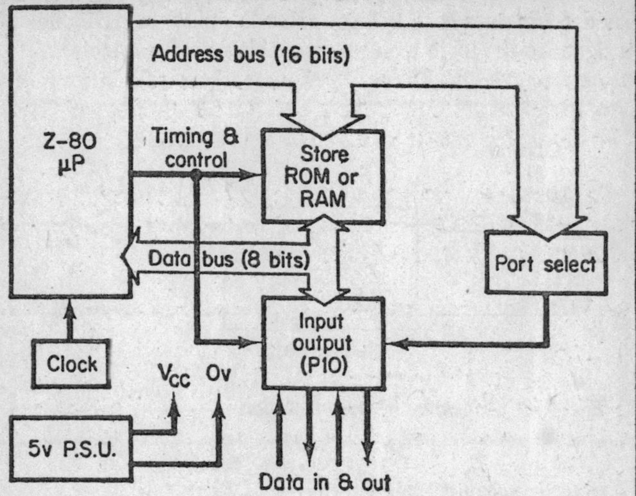

Fig. 4.11 Minimum Z-80 system.

analog or digital form.

Digital inputs will cover items like switches, paper tape readers etc. Digital outputs will include lamps, printers, punch tape, relays etc. Analog inputs occur where an accurate view of some external parameter is required, e.g. thermocouples, sensor positions, throttle settings etc. Analog outputs are necessary where the computer needs fine control, e.g. motor speeds, indicating meters, etc.

With digital inputs and outputs there is really no great problem electronically. In Fig. 4.8 and 4.11 digital signals are connected via suitable gates onto the highway. The only major problem is the avoidance of noise picked up on long interconnecting cables.

This is overcome by the use of optical isolators on inputs and outputs. In Fig. 4.12 we have a battery connected to an LED. In very close proximity we have a phototransistor.

When the LED turns on the light in turn causes TR1 to turn on and the output of IC1 goes to a '1'. We thus have conveyed a signal to the logic with no direct electrical connection.

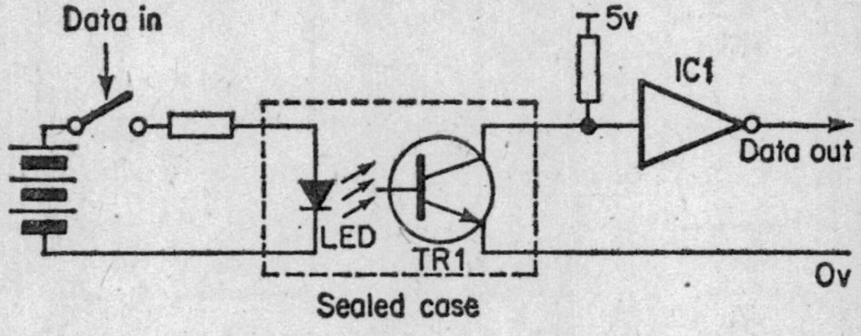

Fig. 4.12 Principles of opto isolation.

A practical circuit is shown on Fig. 4.13. IC1 is an encapsulated opto isolator in a 6 pin D.I.L. package. The output of IC1 is connected to one element of the hex Schmitt trigger IC2. The circuit will work equally well if the battery is replaced by the 10 volt output from the power supply, but this will not show the total isolation attainable.

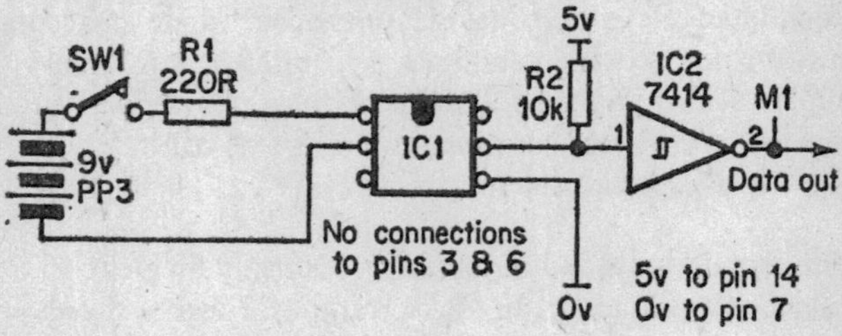

Fig. 4.13 Practical opto isolator.

Digital outputs utilise similar opto isolators, except the computer drives the LED, and the phototransistor connects to the outside world.

Analog signals present more problems. In general, the computer utilises a digital number to represent the analog value (e.g. 0–255 representing 0 to 2.55 volts in 0.01 volt steps). The step size is chosen such that it is smaller than the smallest system resolution, giving effectively a continuously variable signal.

Analog outputs are simplest, so we will deal with that first. The computer outputs a digital number which is converted to an analog voltage by a device called a Digital to Analog Converter, or DAC for short.

Most DACs use a resistor chain to divide a fixed reference voltage to the selected value. A common arrangement is the resistor chain in Fig. 4.14 with the switches implemented by field effect transistors, selected digitally by the computer.

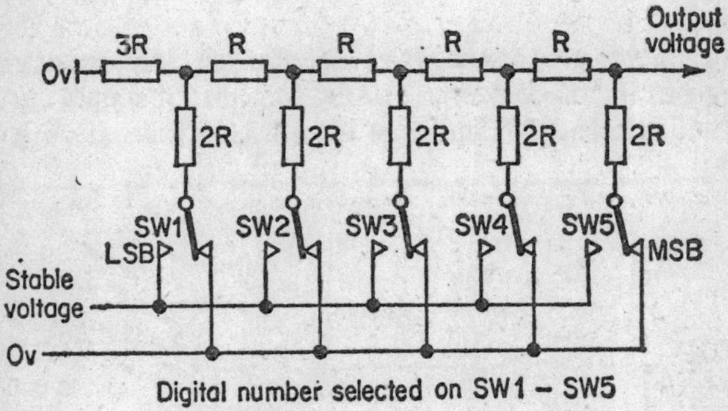

Fig. 4.14 R – 2R resistor DAC.

A typical DAC is the ZN425 i.c.p. shown on Fig. 4.15. This is an 8 bit DAC, with the digital inputs on SW1 – SW8 (SW1 being the least significant) and the analogue output on pin 14. With all 8 bits selected the output voltage is 2.55 volts, so 1 bit = 0.01 volts. The output voltage can obviously be increased to any desired value by amplifiers.

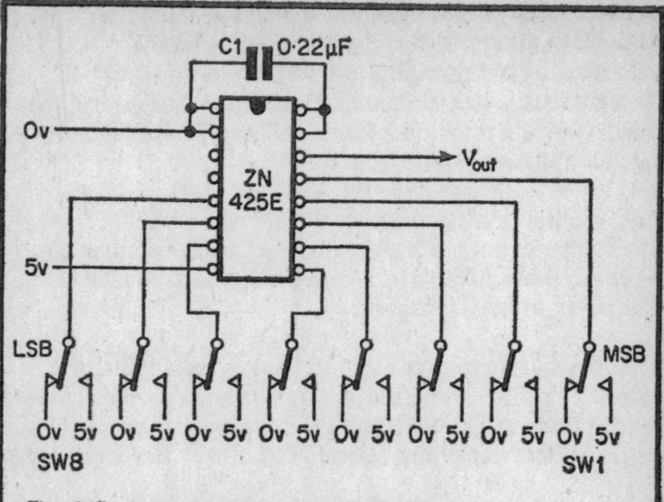

Fig. 4.15 Practical DAC using ZN425E.

Analog inputs are converted to a digital signal by means of an Analog to Digital Converter, or ADC for short. A simple form of ADC is shown on Fig. 4.16. A DAC is driven from a

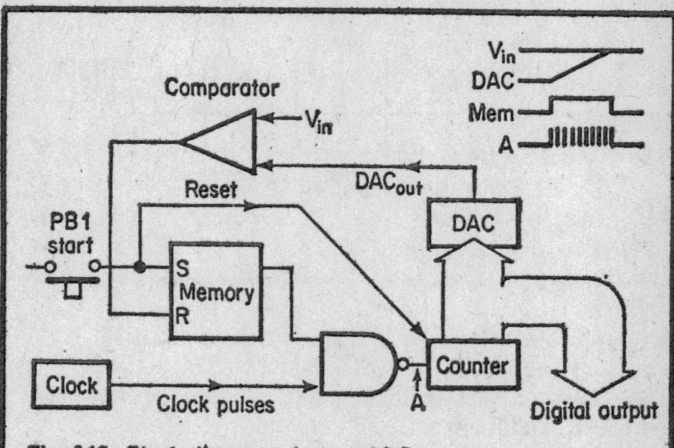

Fig. 4.16 Block diagram of ramp ADC.

counter, so the output voltage is determined by the counter state. When a conversion is required, PB1 sets the flip flop and resets the counter. Clock pulses are now gated to the counter causing it to count up. The output from the DAC is thus a steadily increasing ramp. When the DAC voltage equals the input voltage, the comparator resets the flip flop stopping the counter. The number in the counter now represents the input voltage.

A practical ADC is shown on Fig. 4.17. This again utilises the ZN425 which has an internal counter enabled by pin 2.

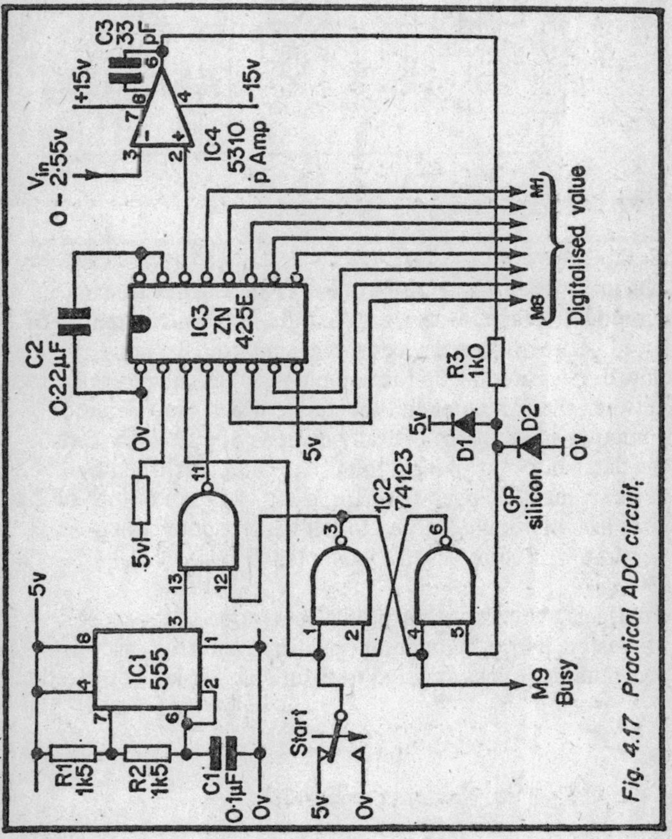

Fig. 4.17 Practical ADC circuit.

A 74132 is used to provide the start memory, and a 555 for the clock. The circuit will work with an input voltage in the range 0 to 2.55 volts, and as before 1 bit represents 0.01 volts. The circuit requires bipolar supply in the range ±6v to ±15v for the comparator. This could be provided by two PP3 batteries or the mains circuit shown on Fig. 4.18.

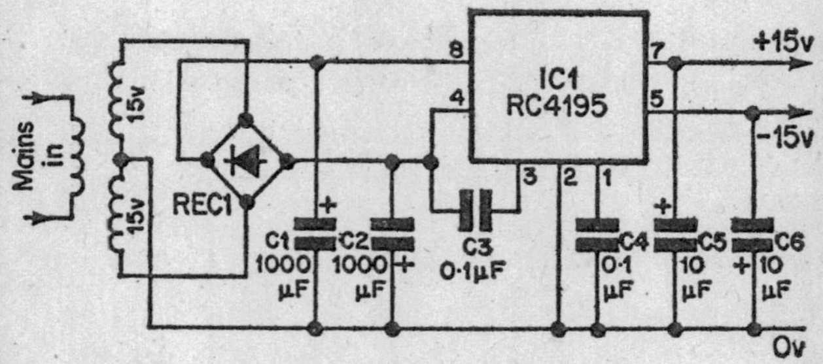

Fig. 4.18 ±15v supply for ADC circuit.

The majority of input/output devices are electromechanical, e.g. printers, tape readers, etc., and there is a vast disparity of speed between these devices and a computer. To prevent these slow devices holding up the computer, interfacing logic is used between the computer and the device which can operate at computer speeds. This basically consists of a latch to store the data, and control logic to tell the computer when the device is ready to operate again. In Fig. 4.17 the output of the start memory could be used to tell the computer when digitisation is complete, for example.

Interfacing with input/output devices is one of the most interesting parts of computer operation, and many clever programming tricks are used to ensure high speed of operation.

5. CONCLUSION

The preceding sections have taken the reader down a long trail from simple gates to the mysteries of computer architecture and input/output interfacing. The reader should now have a good idea of what goes on inside those mysterious black beetle chips called microprocessors.

It is hoped that the reader has found the experiments both interesting and, above all, fun. The next stage now is to obtain a real home computer, and like all computer freaks become totally addicted to one of the most fascinating hobbies in the world.

160	Coil Design and Construction Manual	75p
202	Handbook of Integrated Circuits (IC's) Equivalents & Substitutes	1.00p
205	First Book of Hi-Fi Loudspeaker Enclosures	95p
207	Practical Electronic Science Projects	75p
208	Practical Stereo and Quadrophony Handbook	75p
211	First Book of Diode Characteristics Equivalents and Substitutes	1.25p
213	Electronic Circuits for Model Railways	1.00p
214	Audio Enthusiasts Handbook	85p
218	Build Your Own Electronic Experimenters Laboratory	85p
219	Solid State Novelty Projects	85p
220	Build Your Own Solid State Hi-Fi and Audio Accessories	85p
221	28 Tested Transistor Projects	1.25p
222	Solid State Short Wave Receivers for Beginners	1.25p
223	50 Projects Using IC CA3130	1.25p
224	50 CMOS IC Projects	95p
225	A Practical Introduction to Digital IC's	1.25p
226	How to Build Advanced Short Wave Receivers	1.20p
227	Beginners Guide to Building Electronic Projects	1.25p
228	Essential Theory for the Electronics Hobbyist	1.25p
RCC	Resistor Colour Code Disc	20p
BP1	First Book of Transistor Equivalents and Substitutes	60p
BP2	Handbook of Radio, TV & Ind. & Transmitting Tube & Valve Equiv.	60p
BP6	Engineers and Machinists Reference Tables	75p
BP7	Radio and Electronic Colour Codes and Data Chart	35p
BP14	Second Book of Transistor Equivalents and Substitutes	1.10p
BP23	First Book of Practical Electronic Projects	75p
BP24	52 Projects Using IC741	95p
BP27	Giant Chart of Radio Electronic Semiconductor and Logic Symbols	60p
BP28	Resistor Selection Handbook (International Edition)	60p
BP29	Major Solid State Audio Hi-Fi Construction Projects	85p
BP30	Two Transistor Electronic Projects	1.00p
BP31	Practical Electrical Re-Wiring and Repairs	85p
BP32	How to Build Your Own Metal and Treasure Locators	1.00p
BP33	Electronic Calculator Users Handbook	95p
BP34	Practical Repair and Renovation of Colour TVs	1.25p
BP35	Handbook of IC Audio Preamplifier & Power Amplifier Construction	1.25p
BP36	50 Circuits Using Germanium, Silicon and Zener Diodes	75p
BP37	50 Projects Using Relays, SCR's and TRIACs	1.25p
BP38	Fun and Games with your Electronic Calculator	75p
BP39	50 (FET) Field Effect Transistor Projects	1.25p
BP40	Digital IC Equivalents and Pin Connections	2.50p
BP41	Linear IC Equivalents and Pin Connections	2.75p
BP42	50 Simple L.E.D. Circuits	95p
BP43	How to Make Walkie-Talkies	1.50p
BP44	IC555 Projects	1.75p
BP45	Projects in Opto-Electronics	1.25p
BP46	Radio Circuits Using IC's	1.35p
BP47	Mobile Discotheque Handbook	1.35p
BP48	Electronic Projects for Beginners	1.35p
BP49	Popular Electronic Projects	1.45p
BP50	IC LM3900 Projects	1.35p
BP51	Electronic Music and Creative Tape Recording	1.25p
BP52	Long Distance Television Reception (TV–DX) for the Enthusiast	1.95p
BP53	Practical Electronic Calculations and Formulae	2.25p
BP54	Your Electronic Calculator and Your Money	1.35p
BP55	Radio Stations Guide	1.45p
BP56	Electronic Security Devices	1.45p
BP57	How to Build Your Own Solid State Oscilloscope	1.50p
BP58	50 Circuits Using 7400 Series IC's	1.35p
BP59	Second Book of CMOS IC Projects	1.50p
BP60	Practical Construction of Pre-amps, Tone Controls, Filters & Attn.	1.45p
BP61	Beginners Guide to Digital Techniques	95p
BP62	Elements of Electronics – Book 1	2.25p
BP63	Elements of Electronics – Book 2	2.25p
BP64	Elements of Electronics – Book 3	2.25p
BP65	Single IC Projects	1.50p
BP66	Beginners Guide to Microprocessors and Computing	1.75p
BP67	Counter Driver and Numeral Display Projects	1.75p
BP68	Choosing and Using Your Hi-Fi	1.65p
BP69	Electronic Games	1.75p
BP70	Transistor Radio Fault-Finding Chart	50p
BP71	Electronic Household Projects	1.75p
BP72	A Microprocessor Primer	1.75p
BP73	Remote Control Projects	1.95p
BP74	Electronic Music Projects	1.75p
BP75	Electronic Test Equipment Construction	1.75p
BP76	Power Supply Projects	1.75p
BP77	Elements of Electronics – Book 4	2.95p
BP78	Practical Computer Experiments	1.75p
BP79	Radio Control for Beginners	1.75p
BP80	Popular Electronic Circuits – Book 1	1.95p
BP81	Electronic Synthesiser Projects	1.75p
BP82	Electronic Projects Using Solar-Cells	1.95p